COUNTDOWN TO GCSE:

HISTORY

Nicholas Tate

Senior Lecturer in History,
Moray House College of Education,
Edinburgh

D1457804

M
MACMILLAN
EDUCATION

First published 1986
Reprinted 1986, 1987

Published by
MACMILLAN EDUCATION LTD
Houndmills, Basingstoke, Hampshire RG21 2XS
and London
Companies and representatives
throughout the world

Printed in Great Britain by
Cox & Wyman Ltd
Reading

Designed by
Plum Design
Southampton

British Library Cataloguing in Publication Data
Tate, Nicholas
Countdown to GCSE: History
1. History
I. Title
9000   D21
ISBN 0-333-42253-8

For Emily, Louisa and Oliver

CONTENTS

Countdown to GCSE: History

ACKNOWLEDGEMENTS

The author and publishers wish to acknowledge the following sources:

HMSO for extracts from The National Criteria by permission of the Controller of Her Majesty's Stationery Office; Longman Group Ltd for extract from *Democracy and Reform 1815–1885* by D. G. Wright; Hugh McMillan for extract from 'June Revision'; Macmillan Publishers for extract from *Europe in the 17th Century* by D. Maland (1966); also
London and East Anglian Group; Midland Examining Group; Northern Examining Association; Secondary Examinations Council; Southern Examining Group.

The author and publishers also wish to acknowledge the following photograph sources

Conservative Research Dept.   p 87
Novosti Press Agency   p 14
Vicky/London Express News and Features Services   p 19

The publishers have made every effort to trace the copyright holders, but if they have inadvertently overlooked any, they will be pleased to make the necessary arrangements at the first opportunity.

SECTION I

Introduction to GCSE

WHAT THIS BOOK AIMS TO DO

This book has three main aims:

to tell you what is involved in doing a GCSE History course;
to show you how to do well in such a course;
to suggest what you might do to improve your chances in the exam.

It will also try to convince you that history is an important subject and that it can be very interesting.

All these go together. If you know what your course is trying to do, you'll find it easier to cope with. If you find it interesting, you're more likely to be successful. If you are being successful, it is also much more likely that you will find it interesting.

HOW TO USE THIS BOOK

There are several ways of using this book. The best way is to read all of it fairly quickly as soon as you start your GCSE History course. There are some parts – about objectives (section 2) and about the syllabus (section 3) – that you need to know from the very beginning. At this stage, skip most of the specimen questions and answers in sections 5 and 6.

Come back to these sections once you begin to answer the kinds of questions you will be doing in the exam and study them carefully. Think about what the questions are trying to get you to do. Look closely at the answers that received high marks, and compare your own work with these answers. Make a list of the ways in which your own work might be improved. Concentrate on those types of questions with which you know you have most problems.

Once you start doing the coursework that counts towards your final grade, look again at the advice in section 7. Before planning your final revision, re-read the first two parts of section 4. A few days before the exam, have a quick final glance at the last two parts of section 4.

The other way to use the book is simply to dip into it as you feel the need. The sections are broken up into parts so that you can easily find your way around. At some point, however, you must read section 2, because this explains the basic purposes of a GCSE History course. If you haven't grasped these, you may find some of the things you are asked to do rather puzzling. You should also read the rest of this introductory section, which tells you something about the background to GCSE.

THE GENERAL CERTIFICATE OF SECONDARY EDUCATION (GCSE)

In June 1984, the Secretary of State for Education and Science and the Secretary of State for Wales announced the introduction of a new exam system at 16-plus, to be known as the General Certificate of Secondary Education. The first GCSE exams were to be held in 1988, so courses preparing students for these exams would begin in the autumn of 1986. The new exams would replace the General Certificate of Education 'Ordinary' level (GCE 'O' level), the Certificate of Secondary Education (CSE) and the various joint 'O' level/CSE examinations that had already been introduced. All these other exams would come to an end in 1988.

The government's announcement came after years of discussion and controversy. For a long time many people had been very dissatisfied with the old exam system. It had often been difficult to decide whether someone was more suited to an 'O' level course or to a CSE course. In order to try to overcome this problem, a number of joint 'O' level/CSE exams had been introduced, designed to cater for a much wider range of ability than either 'O' level or CSE on their own. Some of these joint exams had seemed to work quite well, so a lot of the preparation for GCSE had already been done, long before the decision to introduce it was actually announced.

GCSE has the following main features:

1 It is a common system of examining at 16-plus, catering for most of the school population. This means that almost everyone in schools and colleges will be studying for the same certificate.

2 The certificate will be awarded on a seven-point scale: A, B, C, D, E, F and G. At first grades A, B and C will be linked to grades A, B and C of 'O' level and to grade 1 of CSE. Grades D, E, F and G will be linked to grades 2, 3, 4 and 5 of CSE.

'O' level		CSE		GCSE
A	⎫		⎧	A
B	⎬ 'pass'	1	⎨	B
C	⎭		⎩	C
D	⎫ 'fail'	2		D
E	⎬	3		E
		4		F
		5		G

Candidates who don't reach grade G will be ungraded and receive no certificate.

3 GCE and CSE exam boards will work together to run this new exam. They will be divided into five examining groups: the Northern Examining Association (NEA), the Midland Examining Group (MEG), the Southern Examining Group (SEG), and the London and East Anglia Examining Group (LEAG), together with a separate group for Wales called the Welsh Joint Education Committee (WJEC). You can find the addresses of these groups on page 6. The new exam will also be introduced in Northern Ireland. Scotland has a quite separate examination system and will not be affected by these changes. In England and Wales, examining groups will be free to accept entries from schools, colleges and external (or private) candidates from any part of Britain.

4 GCSE syllabuses will be checked to make sure they comply with a long list of regulations about content, methods of assessment and so on. These regulations are both general (i.e. they apply to all subjects), and specific (i.e. they relate to features of particular subjects, such as history). You will be reading quite a lot about these regulations in the rest of this book. They are known as the National Criteria. ('Criteria' simply means 'a set of statements that something has to match up to'.) The General Criteria lay down, for example, that at least 20% of the marks (in all subjects) should be for coursework, i.e. work done in school or college during the course. They also refer to special provision being made for 'external candidates' (candidates not following a course of study at a school or college). This may involve doing an extra exam in place of the coursework.

5 GCSE is designed to be much more of a national exam system than the ones it is replacing. It will therefore be supervised by a national body called the Secondary Examinations Council (SEC). This, for example, will have to approve all GCSE syllabuses, making sure that they match up to the regulations laid down in the National Criteria. The SEC will also keep a check on the actual exams when they are held to make sure that your work is marked as fairly as possible.

THE HISTORY CRITERIA

This book is about GCSE History syllabuses. (A 'syllabus' lists what you have to study in a course.) It is therefore the History Criteria (see 4 above) that we mostly need to look at. All GCSE History syllabuses will have to comply with these Criteria – otherwise they will not get the approval of the SEC.

It is perhaps best to begin with what is *not* laid down by the History Criteria. They do not insist that every History syllabus has to include certain historical topics. There is a great deal of history. All of it is important in one way or another. It was therefore felt to be wrong to insist that certain periods should be studied by *all* students. Apart from anything else, historians would never agree on the most important topics. So GCSE History syllabuses will probably differ more from each other than, say, Mathematics syllabuses. There will be syllabuses on European history, twentieth-century world history, the Tudors and Stuarts, and so on. Most examining groups are likely to offer a number of different syllabuses, and the syllabuses of one examining group will also differ from those of another.

There are certain aspects, however, that all GCSE History syllabuses will have in common. The History Criteria lay down aims and objectives (or purposes) for all GCSE History courses. They specify certain ways in which students are to be assessed, and include rules about how syllabuses are to be put together. You can read more about these features in sections 2 and 3.

The History Criteria also differ from some of the other subject criteria, such as the ones for maths, in that they *don't* insist on different papers for different levels of ability. Examining groups have to produce sets of papers that can be tackled in some way by almost all students, from the very ablest (someone likely to get a grade A) on the one hand, to those who, on the other hand, will have to work hard in order to obtain a grade G. It's up to the groups, however, to decide how best to do this. In practice, no group will be setting different papers in history, because they all feel that it is possible to set common papers for all candidates to attempt. These papers should contain questions that will stretch the ablest, as well as questions that almost everyone ought to answer with some degree of success. They will do this in three main ways.

1 There may be questions of varying difficulty, e.g. some parts of a paper might be fairly easy and other parts much more difficult.

2 Some of the questions may be divided into different parts, beginning with easy sub-questions and ending with more difficult ones. For example:

(a) **List the terms of the Treaty of Versailles.**

(b) **To what extent do you think that Germany was fairly treated by the terms of this settlement?**

The first part *(a)* just asks for a list of terms, so if you have revised this topic carefully, you might be able to answer without a great deal of thought. The second part *(b)*, however, is much more demanding. It requires you to think about all the various terms of the treaty in turn, and to decide whether and in what ways you think they were fair, as well as to assess to what extent you think they were not fair. These are quite difficult skills. Some people who cope well with *(a)* may not cope so well with *(b)*.

3 There may be questions that everyone can attempt, but which give abler candidates the chance to show what they are really capable of doing. For example, a question might ask how a particular piece of historical source material (e.g. a diary or a letter) is or is not useful to the historian. One person might say it was useful because it told you about, say, the life of the poor in the early nineteenth century. Someone else might add that it told you a lot about skilled workers, but nothing about the unskilled. An even better answer might comment that the writer was biased, and that his account might not therefore be an accurate or fair one. The ablest candidate might say all this and also discuss how the historian might be interested in learning about the writer's attitudes, that these told you something about the views of that sort of person at that time, and so on.

There are likely to be a lot of questions like this in GCSE History exams. It is very important to remember that this is how they will be assessed. Some questions may look deceptively simple. They will certainly be phrased in very simple words – often much simpler than in 'O' level, for example. But don't jump to the conclusion that you can dash off the first answer that comes into your head. Think very carefully before you write. Think – and think again. Check your statements against the facts or the evidence. Don't make rash general statements (e.g. *all* Russian nobles beat their peasants, *all* Russian people loved Lenin, etc.). The questions are designed to distinguish between people who forget about such considerations, and those who are thoughtful and cautious and thorough in what they write. These are the abilities that you need to develop, and the rest of the book will show you ways in which you can learn and practise these historical skills.

Exam group addresses

Northern Examining Association, Joint Matriculation Board, Manchester M15 6EU

Midland Examining Group, University of Cambridge Local Examinations Syndicate, Syndicate Buildings, 1 Hills Road, Cambridge CB1 2EU

Southern Examining Group, Southern Regional Examinations Board, Avondale House, 33 Carlton Crescent, SO9 4YL

London and East Anglia Examining Group, University of London School Examinations Board, Stewart House, 32 Russell Square, London WC1B 5DN

Welsh Joint Education Committee, 245 Western Avenue, Cardiff CF5 2YX

SECTION 2
What GCSE History aims to do

AIMS AND ASSESSMENT OBJECTIVES

You read about the National Criteria for History in section 1. They begin by setting out the *aims*, or purposes, of a GCSE History course. Whatever syllabus you are following, it is bound to include each of these aims:

2.1 to stimulate interest in and enthusiasm for the study of the past;

2.2 to promote the acquisition of knowledge and understanding of human activity in the past, linking it, as appropriate, with the present;

2.3 to ensure that candidates' knowledge is rooted in an understanding of the nature and the use of historical evidence;

2.4 to help pupils, particularly in courses on British History, towards an understanding of the development over time of social and cultural values;

2.5 to promote an understanding of the nature of cause and consequence, continuity and change, similarity and difference;

2.6 to develop essential study skills such as the ability to locate and extract information from primary and secondary sources; to detect bias; to analyse this information and to construct a logical argument (usually through the medium of writing);

2.7 to provide a sound basis for further study and the pursuit of personal interest.

Before we see what all this means in practice, have a look as well at the next section of the History Criteria. This lays down the *assessment objectives* of a GCSE History course. These are the things that you (the *candidate*) will be expected to show you can do – in the coursework and in the written examination. You will see at a glance that they follow on from the aims that you have just read.

All candidates will be expected:

3.1 to recall, evaluate and select knowledge relevant to the context and to deploy it in a clear and coherent form;

3.2 to make use of and understand the concepts of cause and consequence, continuity and change, similarity and difference;

3.3 to show an ability to look at events and issues from the perspective
of people in the past;

3.4 to show the skills necessary to study a wide variety of historical
evidence which should include both primary and secondary written
sources, statistical and visual material, artefacts, text-books and
orally transmitted information

    3.4.1 by comprehending and extracting information from it;

    3.4.2 by interpreting and evaluating it – distinguishing between
fact, opinion and judgement; pointing to deficiencies in the
material as evidence, such as gaps and inconsistencies; detecting bias;

    3.4.3 by comparing various types of historical evidence and reach-
ing conclusions based on this comparison.

It will help you make more sense of these aims and objectives if we
group them under four general headings:

Knowledge and understanding;
Concepts;
Empathy;
Skills.

KNOWLEDGE AND UNDERSTANDING

All GCSE History syllabuses will assess you on what you *know* and
understand about the periods or topics you have been studying. Some
will be more concerned with this than others. The London and East
Anglia Examining Group, for example, offers four syllabuses: **A** Modern
World History, **B** British and European History, **C** British Social and
Economic History, and **D** Schools History Project 13–16. In syllabuses **A**,
B and **C** most of the exam questions can't be answered without quite a
lot of background knowledge of the particular topic. This applies to all
the types of questions that are asked: short-answer questions, essays
and questions based on evidence. But in syllabus **D**, one whole paper in
the examination (Paper 2) is based on a topic about which you are
expected to have no knowledge at all. The questions on that paper test
skills rather than knowledge.

    Knowledge means many things. At its simplest, it might involve the
recall (or remembering) of important facts: the Six Points of the
People's Charter of 1838, the European country that ruled Angola
before the 1970s, or the terms of the Trade Union Act of 1927. Some
exam papers will specifically ask you to recall information of this kind.
Even if they don't, these are things you will need to *learn* and *remem-*

ber. Unless you have a lot of correct information at your fingertips, you won't find it easy to answer well many of the questions that you are going to be asked.

By itself, however, knowing a lot of correct facts won't get you very far. That is why the History Criteria refer to *understanding* as well as knowledge. It's no good knowing that one of the Six Points of the People's Charter asked for the abolition of property qualifications for MPs, if you don't understand what 'property qualification' means or why the Chartists wanted it abolished. Most GCSE questions will therefore be testing your understanding at the same time as they are testing your knowledge. You might be asked, for example:

(a) **What were the Six Points of the People's Charter?**
   [knowledge]   *(3 marks)*
(b) **Why were they important to the Chartists?**
   [understanding]   *(4 marks)*

The second of these questions is specifically designed to test assessment objective *3.1*: 'to recall, evaluate and select knowledge relevant to the context and to deploy it in a clear and coherent form'. *Recall* involves remembering a lot of relevant information about the Chartists. *Evaluate and select* means choosing from all this information those bits that will help you answer this particular question – what the basic aims of the Chartists were, why they wanted the secret ballot, what good they thought would come from having annual parliaments, etc. *Deploy ... in a clear and coherent form* means using all this correct and relevant information in order to write an answer to this particular question that is well argued and clearly expressed. Section 5 will give you advice on how best to set about doing this.

There are two other aims concerning knowledge and understanding that are worth looking at. The first of these is that knowledge and understanding of the past should be linked 'as appropriate, with the present' *(2.2)*. The second is 'to help pupils, particularly in courses on British History, towards an understanding of the development over time of social and cultural values' *(2.4)*. These two aims are really saying the same thing – that a course in history should show you the connections between the present and the past. One of the reasons for studying history is to understand the world in which we live today. We can't do this unless we know how this world has come about, and this involves looking at events in the past.

Take, for example, the situation in the Lebanon. This is a country that has become familiar to everyone in recent years. Newspaper head-lines and radio and television news bulletins keep referring to some new crisis there. How much of this news can we understand if we don't know anything about its history? Probably not very much. In order to explain present events in the Lebanon, we need to find out how two separate communities have developed within the same country – Christians and Muslims. This takes us back to the Middle Ages – the spread of the Muslim religion in the Middle East, the attempts by Christians to recover lands that the Muslims had gained, the traditional rivalries between the two groups. More recently, it takes us back to the interwar years, when Christians strengthened their position under French rule, and to the years after 1948 when large numbers of Muslim Palestinian refugees arrived in the Lebanon. Without this background, much of what is happening in the present will seem meaningless. This is just one example. The same is true of the problems of Northern Ireland, relations between the USA and the USSR, and the present state of the British economy. None of these can be understood without knowing a great deal about the past.

What can *you* do to make sure that you satisfy these aims and objectives about knowledge and understanding – both in your course-work and in the exam?

Firstly, you will have to be familiar with a great deal of information. You won't be successful in most history examinations unless you can remember *what* happened, *when* it happened, *where* it happened, and *to whom* it happened. This, by itself, is not enough – history exams are *not* like *Mastermind* or *Top of the Form* – but it will be a good start. The information you'll need to know will depend on the syllabus you are following (section 3) and the kinds of questions you are going to be asked (sections 5 and 6).

Secondly, you will need to *understand* as well as *know* about the periods and topics you are studying. It isn't sufficient to know that the Nazis gained 230 seats in the July 1932 elections or that Hitler became Chancellor in January 1933. You will also need to understand what kind of person Hitler was, what his ideas were, why he won so much support and what were the effects of his coming to power on Germany and the rest of the world. All the time you are studying your GCSE History course, keep on asking questions like these: *why* did this happen? Why was it *important*? What *effects* did it have? *Why* did it have these effects? What is the *meaning* of this word? If you are ever unsure about the answers to any of these questions, don't just give up or assume it is too difficult for you. Ask your history teacher to explain what it is all about. Re-read your notes or text-book. Look up difficult words in a dictionary.

Thirdly, you will need to keep on making connections between the periods you are studying and the present day. This is true of all History syllabuses, but especially those concerned with twentieth-century history. Read a good newspaper, listen to the news on radio or tele-vision, look out for good documentary programmes. If you have been studying the Lebanon, for example, keep up to date with recent developments in that country. Some questions in twentieth-century world history papers ask you to write about events 'up to the present day'. Accurate information about recent developments can sometimes greatly improve the quality of your answers to questions like these.

CONCEPTS

The concepts referred to in this section are those listed in assessment objective *3.2*: 'cause and consequence, continuity and change, similarity and difference'. All GCSE History syllabuses are designed to develop your understanding of these concepts. It is very important therefore that you know what they mean.

A concept is an idea. Let's begin with the concept of a 'cause'. This is the idea that some events 'lead to' or 'cause' other events. Put like that it sounds very simple. You might say, 'I know this already. I don't need a history course to teach me this kind of thing.' On one level you *do* know this already. On another level it isn't quite so simple. Some events seem to have one very obvious cause (e.g. the destruction of the town of Pompeii in AD 79, which was caused by the eruption of the volcano Mt Vesuvius). Others are much more complicated (e.g. the French Revolution or the First World War). With events like these you need to distinguish between major and minor causes, or between short-term and long-term causes. You also need to realise how difficult – and sometimes impossible – it can be to decide what the cause is or whether one cause was more important than another.

Take the outbreak of the French Revolution of 1789, for example. Why did this happen in 1789 rather than 1779 or 1769? Was it a result of the very high bread prices in the summer of 1789? Was it, on the other hand, mainly because the calling of the Estates General had aroused people's hopes? To what extent was it a middle-class revolution, as some have suggested, or is that an over-simplified way of looking at it? How important was the War of American Independence as a long-term cause, e.g. to what extent did France's involvement in that war help to bankrupt the government, and to what extent did it help in spreading new ideas about freedom and equality? These are all questions about *causes*. None of them is easy to answer, but asking them helps you to *explain* why this important event occurred when it did. Questions like these keep on cropping up whenever you do any history. That's why learning to make use of the concept of a cause is regarded as one of the basic objectives of a history course.

The concepts listed in the aims and assessment objectives are linked in pairs. This is because they are like the opposite sides of the same coin. If you are thinking about the causes of an event, you are also thinking about that event as the *consequence* of those causes. High bread prices were one of the *causes* of the peasant revolts that took place in France in the summer of 1789; the revolts were therefore one *consequence* of those high prices. As with causes, however, it isn't quite as simple as it appears. It isn't always easy to decide what the consequences of something were, e.g. whether Germany's harsh treatment at the end of the First World War was the main reason for Hitler's later rise to power. Like causes, consequences can also be both short term and long term. A short-term consequence of Russia's entry into the First World War in 1914 was the mobilisation of large numbers of soldiers. A long-term consequence was the fall of the monarchy and the establishment of a new system of government.

The second pair of concepts is *continuity* and *change*. These also relate to everything you study in history. *Change* is fairly obvious. Throughout history, societies have kept on changing in all kinds of ways. Historians are concerned with *how* these changes have taken place, *why* they have taken place and what *effect* they have had. Changes, however, can be gradual or sudden. They can also be limited or wide-ranging in their effects. Many changes took place in the way of life of British people during the 1920s and 1930s. These were much more gradual and much less far-reaching, however, than the changes that took place in the way of life of most Russian people during the same period. This is where the concept of *continuity* comes in. There are often many aspects of life that do not change, or change very little. Despite all the wars and revolutions and political changes that took place in France, many French peasants were still using farming methods in 1850 that hardly differed from those of 1800. These are just a couple of examples. You can find similar ones in whatever period or topic you are studying. So in studying history, try to become aware of these patterns of continuity and change.

The final pair of concepts is *similarity* and *difference*. In trying to make sense of the past, historians are always comparing one situation with another. They are identifying similarities and differences: the ways in which 'physical force' Chartists had the *same* aims as 'moral force' Chartists, but tried to achieve them by *different* methods; the ways in which the Russian and Chinese revolutions were *similar* (e.g. inspired by Marx's ideas), but also very *different* (e.g. one based in the cities, the other in the countryside). Often we understand much more about one situation or event when we have compared it with another situation or event. Doing this isn't as easy as it might sound, so it is something that you should keep on practising.

A lot of the time you will be making use of all these concepts without realising you are doing so. That doesn't matter. There are two ways, however, in which you can make a conscious effort to satisfy these aims and objectives about concepts.

1 *Don't* study different parts of the course as if they were completely isolated from each other. Try, for example, to see how events in the 1930s have their origins in the First World War. Compare what Disraeli did in his foreign policies with what Gladstone did. Think about the ways in which states in Africa have had different experiences since independence. Students revising for history exams often think of the various parts of their course as quite separate units, with labels like 'Gladstone's foreign policies', 'Disraeli's foreign policies', 'Lenin', 'Stalin', etc. They forget that these labels are just convenient ways of dividing things up. In reality all these people and events are connected with each other in all sorts of ways. Keep on trying to work out what the connections are.

2 In writing about the past, try not to give the impression that everything is simple and clear cut. Candidates in history exams often say things like: 'Lenin and Stalin were totally different from each other in their policies', 'Germany was responsible for the outbreak of the First World War', 'The Chartists were a complete failure.' Statements such as these have one thing in common: they are exaggerated and over-simplified. Lenin and Stalin may have been different in many ways, but they were not *totally* different. Germany may have been partly responsible – or even mainly responsible – for the outbreak of the First World War, but it was not *wholly* responsible, as the statement seems to suggest. The Chartists may have failed in the short term to achieve any of their aims, but that doesn't mean that they were a *complete* failure. If you write like this it will soon become clear to the examiner that you have *not* learnt to 'make use of and understand the concepts of cause and consequence, continuity and change, similarity and difference'. So be cautious. Remember that the events you are studying are often very complex and can't be summed up in simple phrases like 'complete failure' and 'totally different'. Show that you understand this in the way you write.

EMPATHY

This word is probably new to you. You may not even find it in your dictionary. It is quite straightforward, though, and simply means being able to put yourself in the position of other people. Assessment objective *3.3* is the one concerned with empathy: 'to show an ability to look at events and issues from the perspective of people in the past'.

Most GCSE History syllabuses will involve coursework assignments or exam questions specifically designed to test this ability. Even when this is not the main ability being tested, it still helps you make sense of the past if you can see it from the point of view of people who were alive at the time.

Take the men in the photograph, for example. They are Russian soldiers – probably peasants. They have deserted from their army, which at this time (1917) was fighting the Germans in the First World War. They are probably on their way back to their home village. How can we put ourselves in their position, to see events from their perspective?

Firstly, we would have to think about their *feelings* and *motives*. They look happy enough, making their way home to the sound of the accordion. Why might they be happy? What are they looking forward to? What are they glad to have escaped from? Why did they decide to desert? Why did they desert at this time rather than earlier in the war? What would it feel like to walk hundreds of miles? Where might they sleep? What would they have to eat? What problems might they meet in the course of their journey?

Secondly, we would have to think about the *attitudes*, *beliefs* and *opinions* that they might have had. What did they see as the purpose of the war? How did they regard the Tsar (Emperor)? What might they have thought about the various groups of revolutionaries who were trying to win the support of ordinary people at this time? Are they likely to have had strong religious views? What did they think about Russia's system of land ownership?

Once you begin to think about it, there is an awful lot we would need to know in order to put ourselves in their position. Some of it you would get from background information about Russia during the First World War – conditions at the front, the outbreak of the February Revolution, the activities of revolutionaries. You would need to use your *imagination*, however, to apply the information to this particular situation. How might these peasant soldiers have felt when they heard that the Tsar had abdicated? How might they have responded to the officers who tried to discourage them from deserting? What fears might they have had for the future?

All the time you are studying history, you should be using your imagination in this way. It isn't always easy, but it's well worth the effort. Apart from anything else, it makes history much more interesting to try stepping into someone else's shoes (or boots in this case).

It always helps if you can see pictures or photographs of the people you are studying and of the places where they lived. There is not much point in trying to imagine what it would have been like to take part in the storming of the Bastille in 1789 if you don't know what the Bastille looked like (a big fortress), how the soldiers defending it were armed, what sorts of clothes French people wore at that time, and so on. So make sure that you look closely at the illustrations in your history text-books. Check what other illustrated books are available in your school or college library or in the public library. (There are some marvellous books of photographs, for example, that show what life was like in Russia before 1917.) Museums and art galleries may also have exhibitions from time to time that are related to the topics and periods you are studying. Look out for the posters and adverts that announce these. The film *One day in the Life of Ivan Denisovitch* will tell you more about what life was like in a Soviet labour camp than any number of text-books, however good. The same is true of a lot of other films – though some (e.g. the film *Dr Zhivago*, about the Russian Revolution) can also give you a very misleading impression of what conditions were like.

These, then, are some of the things you can do to make sure that you satisfy the assessment objective about empathy. You are more likely to satisfy it if you do two other things as well.

1 Never forget that all the societies you are studying were divided into different groups or classes, and that these groups and classes often had quite different feelings and opinions about life. Most Russian noblemen probably felt very differently about the Russian Revolution from most Russian factory workers. Answers that describe 'the Russian people' as wanting this or doing that, as if everyone felt the same, have got it all wrong. Students writing like this have failed to use their imagination. Make sure you aren't one of them.

2 Never forget as well that, even within a particular group or class, people are bound to differ in their attitudes and views. Some Russian

noblemen were very sad when the Emperor gave up his throne, but some were very pleased, and some even supported the Bolshevik Revolution. Think about your own class at school or college, for example. You might have a lot in common, but you are likely to disagree on all sorts of topics from pop music to politics. So don't write as if *all* French peasants or *all* Russian soldiers always thought and felt the same things. For all we know, the soldier in the photograph with the accordion (page 14) might have been leaving the army in order to take up a musical career. He might not even have heard that a revolution had taken place.

SKILLS

The aims and assessment objectives in the History Criteria refer to a number of *skills*. These are things that you will have to show you are able to *do*, as opposed to things you will have to show that you *know*. The relevant parts are aim *2.6* and assessment objective *3.4* (on pages 7 and 8). Read them again before continuing with this section.

It is probably this aim and this objective more than anything else that make GCSE History courses different from the kinds of courses they have replaced. One of the main reasons for including them is so that you can learn what historians *do* when they study the past.

Notice that both the aim and the assessment objective refer to *sources*. These are what your study of the past is based upon, so it is very important that you know how to use them. Two main kinds of sources are mentioned: *primary* sources and *secondary* sources. A primary source is something that dates from the period you are studying. It could be anything: a letter, a diary, a newspaper, even a painting or an object (an artefact). Whatever it is, it is a primary source if it was written or made during the period you are studying. A secondary source, however, is something that appeared later on – for example a text-book or an encyclopedia, or a book by a modern historian. Both types of sources should play an important part in your course. You should be able, if asked, to distinguish between them, i.e. to say which is primary and which is secondary and for what reasons. You should also be able to make use of them in a number of ways. These are listed in parts *3.4.1, 3.4.2* and *3.4.3* of the assessment objective.

Part *3.4.1* is fairly straightforward. All it is saying is that you should be able to understand the source. To show that you have understood it, however, you will need to write about it. This normally involves explaining *in your own words* what it is saying. It can also involve *summarising* it, i.e. sorting out the important points from the less important. This will require a lot of practice. You will also need to *extract* information from a source to answer a particular question. To do this you will have to *select* the information relevant to that question, ignoring anything that is not relevant.

Part *3.4.2* is concerned with what you do with a source once you have understood what it is saying. The key word here is *evaluate*. It's an off-putting word, but quite clear once you begin to think about it. Take, for example, this modern account of Stalin, the ruler of Russia from 1927 to 1953:

> Stalin had many achievements to his credit. He greatly increased agricultural and industrial production. He helped to make Russia one of the two greatest powers in the world. He provided the leadership needed to hold out against and finally defeat the Germans in the Second World War. None of these achievements, however, excuses the many barbarities committed during his rule: the execution of thousands of so-called 'opponents', the labour camps, the liquidation of the kulaks (richer peasants). When he died in 1953, some Russian people mourned his death. Most must have felt a great sense of relief.

In trying to evaluate this, one of the things you will need to do is 'distinguish between fact, opinion and judgement'. You might indeed be set a question on this passage that asks you to give one example of a 'fact' that it contains and one example of an 'opinion' or a 'judgement'.

Let's begin with the *facts* that it seems to contain. It is clearly a fact, for example, that Stalin died in 1953. To say this involves no opinion or judgement. It is possible that the writer might get this kind of thing wrong and put '1954' or '1952'. That, however, would simply be an incorrect statement of fact. It wouldn't make it an opinion or a judgement. The date of Stalin's death is the most obvious statement of fact in this passage. It is also a fact that he 'greatly increased agricultural and industrial production' (though historians might disagree about how 'great' was 'greatly'), that Russia 'finally defeat[ed] the Germans in the Second World War', and that labour camps were set up during Stalin's rule. These events either happened or they didn't happen. In this case we know they did. These, therefore, are facts.

Does this passage, however, contain statements of *opinion* as well? There are actually quite a lot. The last sentence, for example, is something that the writer cannot know for certain. What 'most' people felt in 1953 would be very difficult to discover – especially in a country like Russia, where people were not free to say or write what they felt and where there were no reliable public opinion polls. The writer may well be right. He may have come to this conclusion after a great deal of thought and study. It is still, however, an opinion that not everyone might accept. Another example of opinion or *interpretation* is the statement that Stalin 'helped to make Russia one of the two greatest powers in the world'. Few people would probably disagree with this, but it could be argued that Stalin didn't do a great deal to help this, that it would have happened anyway, and that it might even have happened despite him rather than because of him. This statement therefore is the writer's interpretation or opinion. It is a very different kind of statement from saying that Stalin 'died in 1953'. It is important that you learn to make this kind of distinction whenever you are using a source (whether it is a primary or, as in this case, a secondary source).

There is another kind of opinion, or judgement, that the writer makes in this passage. This is where he lets us know whether he approves or disapproves of some of the things that Stalin did. This is what the assessment objective means by the word *bias*. Sometimes writers reveal their bias deliberately – they want us to know how they feel about things. This is probably true in this passage. The writer tells us that: 'Stalin had many achievements to his credit.' He also tells us that: 'None of these achievements . . . excuses the many barbarities committed during his rule'. These are not statements of fact. They are not even opinions or interpretations like the others we have looked at. They are telling us what the writer thinks is *good* or *bad* about the way Stalin ruled Russia. An *achievement* is usually a good thing, something that makes life better in some ways. The writer is saying that some of the things Stalin did were for Russia's good. Not everyone would agree with this. He is also saying that these good things are cancelled out to a large extent by the bad things that he calls 'barbarities'. Again not everyone would agree. There are some people who might even argue that it was necessary to kill off the kulaks, that in the long run this action brought benefits to Russia as a whole.

In this passage the writer seems quite clear about how he feels. He tells us quite frankly what his *judgement* on Stalin is. Sometimes, however, writers are not really aware that what they are doing is telling us whether or not they approve of something or someone. Their feelings just come across in the words they choose. One writer, for example, might describe the death of the Russian Emperor and his family in 1918 as their 'massacre' or 'murder'. Another might call it an 'execution'. The choice of words may well tell us something about their feelings towards this event. An 'execution' is something you might feel was necessary and desirable, even if unpleasant. A 'massacre' is clearly something you think is bad or wrong and can't be justified.

When studying historical sources, always try to work out what the writer's views are – the ways in which he or she reveals his or her opinions, makes judgements or shows bias. Knowing that these views are likely to be there is half the battle. Once you *expect* to find them, they will begin to hit you in the eye as soon as you glance at a source. Remember that this doesn't just apply to written sources. The other types of source material listed in the assessment objectives may also tell you as much about the person who made them as they do about the subject with which they are dealing. Look at the cartoon, for example.

'Can't you see? I've got the people behind me!'

The man in the front of the picture is Ian Smith, Prime Minister of Southern Rhodesia at the time the cartoon was published in 1964. The man at the back represents the black majority population of the country. The purpose of the cartoon is not to give us factual information about Southern Rhodesia. It is to show us what the cartoonist feels about Ian Smith and the way he treats the black people in Southern Rhodesia. Read the caption of the cartoon, and then look at how the black man is drawn. The message is very clear: Smith is wrong when he claims he has the support of the people. In fact he is oppressing them, mistreating them, and preventing them from making known their views. We may share the cartoonist's *opinions*, make the same *judgement* ourselves, and show the same *bias*. That doesn't matter as long as we recognise that it is opinion, judgement and bias we are dealing with, and not fact.

What is true of cartoons can also be true of other kinds of visual sources: paintings, posters, films, and even photographs. It can be true of statistical tables. Some of the official Soviet statistics on agricultural production in the 1920s and 1930s tell us more about what the Soviet government wanted people to believe than they do about what was actually happening. It can also be true of the 'orally transmitted information' mentioned in the assessment objective. These are people's spoken memories of the past. We all know how easy it is to remember things as being different from how they really were. People's 'memories' sometimes tell us more about how they feel *now* than about how they felt *then*. In other words they tell us more about present *opinions* than past *facts*.

So far we have just looked at ways of handling single sources. Part *3.4.3* of the assessment objective also refers to comparisons between 'various types of historical evidence'. Many GCSE exam papers contain questions based on a whole group of sources related to a particular topic, and you can see some examples of questions like this in section 6. These questions test your ability to compare one source with another. You might be asked to identify which of a number of sources was written by a democrat. You might also have to compare two or three versions of the same event. Look at these two accounts of the battle of Lexington (1775) which took place between the British and the Americans at the beginning of the War of American Independence. Notice *three* ways in which they give a different account of the same event.

Account A (by an officer in the British army)

The troops received no interruption in their march until they arrived in Lexington, a town eleven miles from Boston, where there were about 150 rebels (drawn out in divisions, with intervals as wide as the front of the divisions). The light infantry who marched in the front halted and Major Pitcairn came up immediately and cried out to the rebels to throw down their arms and disperse, which they did not do. He called out a second time, but to no purpose; upon which he ordered our light infantry to advance and disarm them, which they were doing when one of the rebels fired a shot. Our soldiers returned the fire and killed about fourteen of them; there was only one of the 10th light infantry received a shot through his leg. Some of them got into the church, but were soon driven out.

Account B (by an officer in the American militia)

I, John Parker, of lawful age and commander of the Militia in Lexington, do testify and declare that on the nineteenth of April, being informed that a number of regular troops were on their march from Boston, ordered our Militia to meet on the Common in said Lexington, to consult what to do, and concluded not to meddle or make with the said regular troops (if they should approach) unless they should insult us; and upon their sudden approach, I immediately ordered our Militia to disperse and not to fire. Immediately said troops made their appearance, and rushed furiously, fired upon and killed eight of our party, without receiving any provocation therefore from us.

Did you notice what the three differences were?

  (a) They disagree about the number of men killed in the fighting.
  (b) They disagree about who fired first.
  (c) They disagree about whether the British troops ordered the Americans to lay down their arms.

If you managed to do this, you satisfied the assessment objective that requires you to 'point . . . to deficiencies in the material as evidence, such as . . . inconsistencies'.

Comparing different pieces of evidence can also involve finding out how they agree as well as how they disagree. If two or more reports say that something took place, then it is likely that it actually did happen – assuming of course that the reports were made independently of each other. In this case both reports tell us that the British troops were on their way from Boston, that a battle took place at Lexington, and that some American soldiers were killed in the fighting. As the two accounts were given independently of each other, we can be much more confident that these things actually happened.

Whether you are handling groups of sources or just looking at a single source, you will also need to consider the *usefulness* of the source or sources to a historian. In the case of the two sources about Lexington, you might say that they were both useful because they were eyewitness accounts (i.e. their authors were actually present at the battle). They were also written or spoken shortly afterwards (i.e. while they were still fresh in the authors' minds). These are *strengths* of the sources. On the other hand, both the British and the American officers had reasons for wanting their own side to appear in the best possible light. Their accounts therefore disagree with each other and it isn't easy to decide which one to believe. These are *weaknesses* of the sources. This is just one example, but most sources can be looked at in a similar way.

Apart from all this, what more can you do to satisfy the aims and objectives related to skills?

1 You can become familiar with the *types* of primary sources available for particular topics. For the eighteenth-century agricultural revolution, for example, you should be aware that the primary sources include enclosure maps, Acts of Parliament, published books, letters and estate papers.
2 You can think in general terms about the strengths and weaknesses of different types of primary source, e.g. the way photographs sometimes leave out things the photographer doesn't want you to see, or the value of private diaries in which the writer is only concerned with

recording accurately what happened. Exam questions will usually be about the strengths and weaknesses of *particular* primary sources. You will have an advantage, though, if you have thought in advance about the *general* strengths and weaknesses of the types of source.

3 Remember your historical skills when you are reading the daily newspaper, watching a film or TV programme, listening to the radio, or looking at advertisements. Watch out for *propaganda* (one-sided presentation of material), and bias and opinion. Look at the ways in which people's attitudes are revealed. Notice how they disagree and sometimes contradict each other. These things didn't just happen in the past. They are part of our lives today.

You might have noticed that the two aims we have not looked at so far are the first and last ones: 'to stimulate interest in and enthusiasm for the study of the past'; and 'to provide a sound basis for further study and the pursuit of personal interest'. These are perhaps the most important aims of all. If your GCSE History course doesn't manage to do this, it will have failed. Whether it fails or succeeds will depend partly on how you are taught, but above all, it will depend on *you*. All the people who have been involved in planning the courses very much hope that you *will* find history interesting. They also hope that you will want to carry on finding out about it after school. History is very varied. It can also be very exciting – and it's about real people. Without it, we can't understand the world we live in today. If you do enjoy the subject, your *interest* and *enthusiasm* will come across in how you write. Apart from anything else, this is bound to give you a better chance of doing well in your coursework and in the examination.

SECTION 3

The syllabus: What you need to know and understand

DIFFERENCES BETWEEN SYLLABUSES

The aims and objectives you read about in the last section are the same for all GCSE History courses. The actual syllabus, however, will vary from one course to another. Different syllabuses will involve the study of quite different periods and topics. It is up to your school or college to choose which History syllabus to follow. As you learned in section 1, each examining group may offer a number of History syllabuses. Even syllabuses with the same name – e.g. 'Twentieth-Century World History' – may be very different from each other once you begin to look at what they actually include.

As well as their aims and objectives, all syllabuses will have certain other features in common. These are laid down in the History Criteria. This is what the Criteria say:

In order to allow the assessment objectives to be realised, syllabuses must satisfy the following criteria:

4.3.1 **they must be of sufficient length, range and depth;**
4.3.2 **they must deal with key issues;**
4.3.3 **they must be historically coherent and balanced.**

It will be clear what is meant by *4.3.1* and *4.3.2*. History syllabuses must involve the study of quite a long period of time. This must be long enough for you to look at both the long-term causes of change and at its long-term effects (*length*). Syllabuses must also look at more than just one aspect of life during the chosen period (*range*). They must involve some study in depth, so that you can really get to grips with learning what life was like at a particular time (*depth*). And, finally, they must be concerned with developments that have been of great importance in the history of the countries involved, e.g. the Industrial Revolution or the First World War (*key issues*). The History Criteria

23

give examples of how a number of syllabuses satisfy these criteria. This is for a syllabus on 'British Social and Economic History 1760-1914':

This syllabus is of sufficient *length* to allow study, for example,

1 of population change in periods of slow and rapid growth;
2 of agriculture during prosperity and depression;
3 of development of communications over the period.

The criterion of *range* will be satisfied, as the syllabus should include economic (e.g. changes in government policy concerning taxation and trade), social (e.g. attitudes and policy about poverty and public health) and technological aspects (e.g. impact of inventions in the textile industry). Political aspects (such as the widening of the franchise and local government growth), religious and cultural developments (exemplified in attitudes to education and involvement in philanthropic movements) and scientific changes (such as the impact of Pasteur's work on medical and public health practices) could all be included. The importance of world trade and the impact of foreign competition should be studied so that British developments are fitted into a wider context.

In a syllabus of this length and range it is not necessary to study topics in considerable depth, as long as the combined effect of studying the various aspects gives a sufficiently detailed picture of the overall changes which take place.

In selecting specific topics, syllabuses should look to *key issues*, for example, in industrial and technological development, the textile and iron and steel industries; in studying popular political movements, Chartism; in religious aspects, Methodism and the Salvation Army.

These criteria can be met by all sorts of different syllabuses. Under the surface they may have all these things in common, but in practice they will look very different. These are the six main types of syllabuses that will be offered. Some examining groups may not offer all six types.

1 Syllabuses concerned with aspects of *British* history or (before 1707) with *English* history. Most of these are likely to concentrate on the period between the middle of the eighteenth century and the present day. Some groups, however, may offer syllabuses on the medieval, and Tudor and Stuart periods.
2 Syllabuses concerned with aspects of *European* history. Again, most of these are likely to concentrate on the period between the middle of the eighteenth century and the present day.
3 Syllabuses in which it is possible or necessary to study aspects of both *British and European* history.
4 Syllabuses concerned with aspects of *British social and economic history*. Most of these are concerned with the period between the middle of the eighteenth century and the present day.

24

5 Syllabuses concerned with *twentieth-century world history*.
6 Syllabuses based on the *Schools History Project 13-16*. This
Project has five main parts: a study of a topic (e.g. medicine) over a
very long period of time; a detailed study of a limited period (e.g.
Britain 1815-51); a study of topics in modern history (e.g. Modern
China); a local historical study; a study of the methods used by the
historian (linked closely to the other four parts of the syllabus).

Not all syllabuses may fit easily into these six types, but it is very
likely that you will be following one of them. Within each type there
will also be big differences between one syllabus and another. Some
syllabuses on world history, for example, will be divided into themes.
The Modern World syllabus offered by the NEA is divided into 'five
broad themes'. These are:

1 *Conflict and conciliation;*
2 *Governments in action;*
3 *International cooperation;*
4 *Colonialism;*
5 *Human rights.*

Each of these themes is described in some detail. This is what you have
to study for one of the four parts of Theme 1:

1 Conflict and conciliation

... *(b)* **The Changing Nature of Warfare**

(i) **The Western Front 1914-18:**
trench warfare - its character and physical and psycho-
logical effects; changing attitudes to war.

(ii) **Developing techniques of warfare in World War Two:**
Blitzkrieg; Battle of Britain; bombing campaigns; Stalin-
grad; Pearl Harbor; Submarine warfare; D-Day Landings
and Liberation of France; Hiroshima.

(iii) **The Cold War and Nuclear Arms Race:**
crises in Berlin, Hungary, Cuba, Czechoslovakia; the
Nuclear Arms Race.

(iv) **Guerrilla Warfare in Vietnam:**
the Vietcong, its objectives and methods; US response; the
outcome.

By contrast, the London and East Anglia Examining Group divides
up its twentieth-century world history syllabus into sections concerned
with the different regions of the world (though there is also an optional
section on international themes). These regions are Asia; Africa south
of the Sahara; the Middle East and North Africa; Latin America and the
Caribbean; North America; Western Europe including Britain; the Soviet
Union and Eastern Europe. You do not have to study all of these

regions. As in the NEA syllabus, the topics you have to study for each region are given in detail. These, for example, are the topics for Asia:

Section A: Asia

Reasons for and course of Japanese aggression during the 1930s. The main events of the war in the Far East, 1941–45. The British presence in the Indian subcontinent; the response to colonialism; political divisions leading to partition in 1947. Main features of the subsequent history of India and Pakistan, including the creation of Bangladesh. China during the interwar years; reasons for and events leading to the establishment of Communist rule in China. The consolidation of Communist control and the nature of Communist rule during the time of Mao Tse-tung; internal developments since the death of Mao. Communist China's relations with other powers. The decline of European colonialism in South-East Asia; warfare in Korea and Vietnam. The revival of Japan during the years since the Second World War.

You can see how much detail is included in these syllabus regulations. This is to help *you*. By studying the syllabus, you can find out exactly which aspects of a topic or period you have to cover. It is vital that you have this information, and your school or college should tell you about all this. You can also find syllabus details (for all subjects) in the published regulations issued each year by exam groups. These are usually available in public reference libraries, or you might be able to buy them from your exam group (see page 6).

THINGS TO NOTICE IN YOUR SYLLABUS

In studying the regulations for your particular syllabus, there are a number of things you need to notice.

1 Make sure you are clear about the *choices* that have to be made within your syllabus. There are few syllabuses where you have to study all sections in order to complete the course. These are the choices available in the LEAG Modern World History Syllabus referred to above:

Candidates to study *three* of the following sections; *one* chosen from Sections A, B, C or D, *one* chosen from Sections E, F, G or H, and *one other* chosen from either group. This requirement is to ensure that, in following a course on twentieth-century world history, candidates study regions that differ widely from each other in a number of respects.

This means, for example, that you can study Asia (Section A), North America (Section E) and Western Europe including Britain (Section F). On the other hand, you could study Africa south of the Sahara (Section

B), Latin America and the Caribbean (Se ...
themes (Section H). What you don't have to c ...
2 Find out also whether or not you have to be
of each of the sections you are following. This m ...
bus to another. It will depend partly on how
examined on these sections. In the LEAG Moo ...
syllabus, for example, Part 1 of Paper 1 of the exar ...
answer *all* ten questions in the three sections for which ...
prepared. These questions may be on any of the topics .   ...at
section. To make sure you can answer all these questions, y   ...l need
to be familiar with all the topics. In this case it is essential that, in
studying and revising for the exam, nothing is left out. With some GCSE
exams, however, there may always be a choice of questions. In these
cases it won't be quite so essential that you study every part of the sections for which you are being prepared. You may still of course not
want to miss anything out – just to make sure you have as wide a choice
as possible.

3 Make sure you have a good idea about how much *detail* you will
need in the various sections of the syllabus you are studying. You can't
always tell this from the syllabus by itself. The syllabus will tell you,
for example, that you have to study 'The Spanish Civil War, 1936-9'. It
may be difficult, however, to decide how much detail you will need to
know about, say, the military events of this war.

4 Find out how each part of the syllabus is going to be *assessed*. This
may well influence the way you take notes and the way you revise for
the exam. If the assessment for a section is just in the form of essays,
you are likely to revise for that section in a different way from a section where you are mainly assessed on your use of source material. The
kind of assessment used in each section should be spelled out in the
syllabus regulations. This is an extract from the 'scheme of assessment'
used in three of the LEAG syllabuses:

PAPER 1   (1¾ hours)

**Paper 1 is in two parts. This paper will be weighted at 45% of the total
subject marks.**

Part 1 **(weighted at 20% of the total marks) comprises short-answer/
objective questions and is intended primarily to test Objective 1 – the
development of historical knowledge and understanding. There will be
three main types of question in Part 1 in roughly equal proportions:**

   multiple choice,
   writing a sentence,
   one-word answer.

Approximately ¼ of the questions in Part 1 will be based on a variety of

(weighted at 25% of the total marks) comprises structured essay questions and is intended primarily to test Objective 3 – the ability to construct and communicate a simple historical argument. Candidates will be advised to spend about 70 minutes on Part 2.

It is intended that Parts 1 and 2 will be sat in a single session without a break. The answers to Part 1 will be written in the question booklet itself which must therefore be handed in at the end of the examination. The answers to Part 2 will be written in a separate answer booklet or on answer sheets.

PAPER 2 (1½ hours)

This paper will be weighted at 25% of the total subject marks.

Paper 2 comprises evidence questions and is intended primarily to test Objective 2 – the ability to evaluate and interpret evidence. A variety of types of evidence will be used. Usually, each question will comprise a series of sub-questions based on one or more pieces of historical evidence. The total mark available for each sub-question will be shown. Although the sub-questions will be based on the evidence given and will require careful study of that evidence, there will also be one or two sub-questions based not just on the evidence given, but on the student's wider knowledge and understanding of the topic and/or on the student's ability to place the evidence in a historical context or to comment on the value or otherwise of the evidence to the historian.

Even where the syllabus regulations are not as precise as these, you should be able to work out from specimen and past papers exactly what form the assessment is going to take. Remember that some sections of the syllabus may be assessed just by coursework. This again may affect how you plan your work.

5 Make sure you know what *proportion of marks* goes to each part of the syllabus. Notice how the LEAG scheme of assessment that you have just read tells you the proportions of marks for each of: Paper 1; Paper 1, Part 1; Paper 1, Part 2; and Paper 2. (The remaining 30% of marks are awarded for coursework.) It is very important that you have this information. It would be foolish to spend three-quarters of the time available for revision on part of the syllabus that only receives 15% of the marks. You are not likely to do this if you know well in advance what each part of the examination is worth.

It will help again here if you can get hold of specimen or past papers. Your school or college will have copies of these, or you may be able to buy them by writing direct to the exam group (see page 6). Look at the questions. Check how much time you are given. Look at the number of marks awarded for different questions. All this should give you a better idea of how much detail is going to be required. Sometimes you still won't be too sure. In that case always over-prepare rather than under-prepare. Even if it seems that you don't need a lot of the detailed knowledge you have acquired, some of it may still be useful, e.g. as illustrations of general points in essays.

SECTION 4

How to prepare for the exam

Preparation for the exam does *not* begin just a few weeks before you actually take it. It begins on the first day you start your GCSE History course. This doesn't mean you have got to be obsessed with exams and exam questions, because that would make your course very boring indeed. What it does mean is that you should put a lot of effort into every part of the course, bearing in mind all the suggestions made in section 2. GCSE History exams test knowledge, understanding and skills that will have developed gradually over a long period of time. There's still a lot you can do during the last few months before the exam, but if you have done very little up to that point it may be too late.

STUDY HABITS

One way in which you can help yourself, well in advance, to prepare for the exam is by giving some attention to developing the right study habits. It's always very difficult to advise people how best to study. Some people seem to be able to get on with their work despite, or even because of, all the noise around them. Other people can only work in total silence. Some people seem to need short breaks every quarter of an hour – for drinks of coffee or raids on the biscuit barrel. Others can only work well if they have long periods without any kind of break or distraction. Some people can sunbathe in the garden *and* concentrate on reading about the French Revolution. Others usually fall asleep or decide that soaking up the sun is much more important than revising for history exams. Only *you* will know how and where you work best. You'll need to think about it, though, and plan your study time so that you work to best advantage. Some people spend evening after evening half studying and half watching a film on television or half studying and half talking to the rest of their family. They do neither thing properly. They feel irritated because they haven't got very far with their studies. They never really understand what's happening in the film – and the family gets exasperated because they don't reply to questions, only half join in conversations, and so on. A bit of thought and a bit of planning (e.g. 7.00–8.30 p.m., work in my bedroom; 8.30–10.30 p.m., watching

TV film) will make you feel that no part of an evening has been wasted (assuming the film wasn't too awful).

As well as trying to improve your study habits, bear in mind the following pieces of advice. These apply to everyone, whether they work best on the beach, at 2 a.m., or on the upper deck of a bus.

1 Make sure the *notes* you take during the course are always full, clear and easy to read. You may well need to revise from these later on. Write legibly. Put headings - and underline them (e.g. in red) so that they stand out at a glance. Finish off work you weren't able to complete in class or that you missed because you were ill. If your notes are in exercise books you may well have half a dozen of these by the end of the course. Don't lose them. Label each cover, so that you can tell at a glance where the information you need can be found. Stick in at the most appropriate points any handouts that your teacher has given you during the course - or put them in a separate folder. Don't leave them lying around in your desk or locker or in your bag. They will have been lost or folded into a hundred creases by the time you need them for revision. If you use a ring-file, make sure you put your sheets in the right order. Fix them with ring reinforcements (around the holes) if they begin to come loose.

2 If you don't understand the *meaning* of a word you come across, look it up *immediately* in your dictionary, or in the glossary (list of words) or index in your text-book. It can be very useful to build up a list of new words that you have learnt at the back of your exercise book or on a separate page in your file. Refer to this when you come to revise for the exam.

3 If you don't know where a *place* mentioned in your text-book is, try to find it *immediately* on a map. Most text-books have good maps. You may also have a historical atlas - these can be very useful. It's surprising how ignorant some people are about even well-known places. Anyone can avoid this just by a bit of extra effort.

4 If you don't understand *any part* of the course - whether it's a word that someone has used or something much more basic, like why Marx didn't think Russia would be the first country to have a socialist revolution - *ask your teacher to explain*. It's amazing how many people just don't do this. As a result they get more and more confused the further they get into the course. Everyone fails to understand something at some point or other, so there is no reason to feel ashamed to admit it. It's the people who ask and ask again until they are quite clear about something who are the really clever ones.

5 Don't rush homework when you are asked to *read* a chapter or part of a chapter in the text-book or topic books you are using for the course. Reading and re-reading these books is one of the best ways of deepening your knowledge and understanding of the topics covered by the syllabus. Normally you should be able to borrow all these books for revision. Sometimes, however, history departments are so short of money that there aren't enough sets of books to go round. You may well find that you can't take a particular book home with you. This ought not to happen – but sometimes it does. It may even be worth saving up the money to buy your own copy of the book or asking a relative to get you one for a birthday present. Take a note of the title, author and publisher and order it through your local bookshop.

Like the suggestions in section 2, these are all things you should be doing throughout your course. Towards the end of the course, however, you will also need to *revise*. This requires further thought.

REVISION

At some point during the last two terms before your exam, you'll need to start planning your revision programme. What this will involve depends on how many subjects you will be taking in the exam, what these subjects are and how good you are at each of them. Only you will know all this, so only you can work out your revision programme. It's a good idea to put it down on paper. This will help you avoid the panicky feeling that comes over some people before exams – the feeling that there is so little time and so much to revise that you might as well give it all up. Having a plan down on paper makes the whole thing seem much more manageable. You begin to feel in control of the situation and able to cope. This is an example of the kind of plan you might use for part of the Easter holidays immediately before your GCSE exams:

Monday:	geography (area studies – W. Europe)
Tuesday:	geography (area studies – W. Europe)
Wednesday:	geography (water resources – second revision)
Thursday:	history (Asia – China to 1949; Japan to present day)
Friday:	history (Asia – China from 1949; practice questions from past papers)
Saturday (a.m.):	maths (revise book 5)
Saturday (p.m.):	free

Be realistic. Make sure you give yourself enough time for each of these things. Remember that not all subjects require the same amount of revision. History often takes up a lot of time – mainly because there is usually a great deal to be learnt, but some syllabuses may need less revision than others. These are likely to be syllabuses with a big course-work element and syllabuses where the exam questions don't require you to refer all the time to your own knowledge. Wherever possible, allow slightly more time than you think you might need. The plan is bound to have to be altered in various ways, so the more flexible it is the better.

In drawing up your revision programme, allow more time for those parts of the syllabus where you know you are weakest. By the spring term before your GCSE exams, you should have a good idea what these are. Think carefully about how you managed with the various parts of the mock exam. Were you perhaps fairly confident about the Asia section, but less sure about the questions on the Russian Revolution? Did you get good marks for the short-answer questions in Paper 1, but have a lot of problems with the source-based questions in Paper 2? Look back at your essays and other marked pieces of work. What were you good at? Where did you have problems? Asking questions like these should help you decide which parts of the syllabus require the most attention in your revision programme.

What should you actually be doing, though, when you revise? This will again depend on your syllabus, but is likely at some point to include each of the following.

1 Making *summaries* of the main points you need to remember for particular topics. This might involve summarising a wide range of material, including your own notes and essays, worksheets, and sections of your text-books.

There are two reasons for making these summaries. The first is that it helps you absorb, understand and learn the material you are summarising. (After making a summary, you should be much clearer about the main points in a topic.) The second reason is that it provides you with a useful list of points that you will be able to use for a quick revision during the last couple of days before the exam. Some people write their summaries on index cards with headings like 'Stalin (domestic) *1*' or 'Whig reforms *2*' to show at a glance what they are about.

In making your summaries, save time and space by writing in note form. Put down the main points, ignoring details that simply illustrate these or pad them out. Organise these main points under clear, bold headings which are underlined to make them stand out. Read the following passage from a book about seventeenth-century Europe. The chapter from which it is taken refers to Portugal and Spain.

In 1636 Olivares [Spain's chief minister] ordered the collection of a 5 per cent tax on property, a tax hitherto confined to Castile. This provoked a rebellion, but without Braganza's leadership it was so disorganised as to be easily suppressed. Olivares and Vasconcellos were therefore encouraged to pursue their plans further. In 1640 they proposed to abolish the Portuguese Cortes, to enlist the nobles into the Castilian army, and to absorb the kingdom wholly into Castile. So great was the fury that within three hours of the proclamation a revolutionary group had murdered Vasconcellos, seized control of Lisbon and called upon Braganza to become King. In this crisis the decisive figure was Braganza's Spanish wife. Before the day was out Braganza had proclaimed himself King John IV of Portugal. As a further stroke, the Queen persuaded her brother, the Duke of Medina Sidonia, to raise his own standard in Andalusia and to proclaim his province's independence of the Spanish king.

Now read this summary of the passage, and notice how brief it is. Notice too how it highlights the main points and organises them under clear headings.

Summary: Portugal regains independence (1640)
Portuguese *discontent*: new tax (1636 revolt); Spanish attempt (Olivares & Vasconcellos) to abolish Cortes (parliament) in 1640. *Revolt* in Lisbon. Braganza (Port. royal family) proclaimed king. Braganza's Spanish wife very important – also encourages her brother to cause trouble in Spain itself (Andalusia proc. independent).

In making notes, you might find it helpful to use abbreviations, as in the summary above. As long as you always use the same ones, this won't cause any confusion. In fact it will save you a lot of time. Other examples are: Fr. (French), It. (Italian), G's reforms (Gladstone's reforms), HR (Home Rule), GS (General Strike), Nap. III (Napoleon III).

2 Make sure you know the *meanings* of all the words you come across in making your summary. If you haven't built up a glossary (or list) of special terms during the course, do so now. It might include words such as *Cortes* (parliament in Spain/Portugal), as in the passage above; *corvée* (forced labour on roads – in France before 1789); *zemstva* (local councils introduced into Russia by Alexander II); *Darwinism* (ideas about evolution associated with Charles Darwin).

3 Look up all the *places* mentioned in your course on a historical map. If you don't have a separate historical atlas, pay particular attention to the maps that are included in your text-book. Apart from preparing you for questions that might ask you to name places on a map, this will also help you to *understand* much better what the topic involves. Take, for example, the German government's plans for a railway from Berlin to Baghdad just before the First World War. Unless you have looked at the map and seen where such a railway would have had to run, you won't be able to understand why the scheme was unpopular with both the Russians and the British.

4 *Practise* answering questions from past or specimen papers. If you don't have any questions to practise on, ask your teacher if he or she

can supply you with some. If all else fails, you ~~can~~
attempt at questions you have already tackled du~~ring~~
ing there's room for improvement — which there ~~is~~
exam has taken place, you can normally buy past pap~~ers from~~
groups (see page 6).

Make sure that you get practice in answering all the ~~ques~~
tions you are likely to come across. Go through the specime~~n~~
make a list of the different kinds you will have to answer. Th~~ese vary~~
from one syllabus to another. They might include short-answ~~er~~ ~~ques-~~
tions (of various types, e.g. multiple choice, filling in blanks in sentences),
stimulus questions, source-based questions (of various types), and essays
(again of various types). You should know from your work during the
course which kinds you need to practise most.

Practice can involve two things: answering questions in full, as you
would in the actual exam, and working out answer plans. It is useful to
do both. Short-answer questions and some source-based and stimulus
questions require very brief answers. It is better to write these out in
full. With essays, and with some of the longer questions based on a
source or a stimulus, it is often helpful just to work out a *plan*. This
should cover all the main points you would want to include, in the
order in which you would use them (and perhaps indicate how these
points would be grouped into paragraphs). Here is an example of an
answer plan for a question on the Paris peace settlement at the end of
the First World War.

(a) **Describe the terms of the Paris peace settlement with regard to
Germany.**

(b) **To what extent would you agree that these terms were both fair
and wise?**

Plan

(a) Introduction: a dictated peace

Paragraph 1: War guilt clause – reparations/revenues from
Saarland

Paragraph 2: Military restrictions: size of armed forces
(different branches), no conscription, demili-
tarisation of Rhineland (inc. armies of occup-
ation)

Paragraph 3: Loss of territory: in the west (Alsace &
Lorraine; Eupen & Malmédy; plebiscite in
Schleswig)

Paragraph 4: Loss of territory: in the east (Danzig & Polish
Corridor; Memel; E. Prussia surrounded; plebi-
scite in Silesia; forbidden to unite with
Austria)

...xtent ... fair ... wise

Paragraph 5   *Fair* – was Germany guilty? (yes, but . . .)

Paragraph 6:   *Fair* – reparations very harsh. Affecting many Germans who couldn't be held responsible for what their govt. did in 1914

Paragraph 7:   *Fair* – idea of self-determination not always upheld (e.g. Alsace-Lorraine; Polish Corridor; Anschluss with Austria)

Paragraph 8:   *Wise* – not harsh enough to prevent Germany from becoming a great power again

Paragraph 9:   *Wise* – *but* caused great resentment and led to economic collapse of 1923, which (in the long term) helped the rise to power of Nazis (and thus led to WW2)

Paragraph 10:   *Wise* – on other hand, the settlement would have worked if later allied statesmen had enforced it

Treaties were wise; later statesmen (e.g. Chamberlain) were not

This is only one way of answering the question. There are quite a few other ways – especially in part *(b)* where, to some extent, you are asked for your own opinions. However you decide to tackle it, your plan should be brief and clear, and should help you make sure that all the major points have been included. It should make you think about the question (i.e. what points are relevant and what points are not relevant) and should give you useful practice in dividing answers into paragraphs. Writing essay plans is also a skill you will need in the actual exam. You may not, in the exam, have time to work out a plan as detailed as this one, but you should be able to jot down the main points and arrange them in some sort of order. Doing this will actually save you time in the long run – as well as making you feel much more confident once you begin to write.

Sometimes it is also helpful to write out your answer in full – especially if it is a type of question with which you have had problems during the course. Once you have done most of your revision, you might find it useful to answer some of these questions under exam conditions. Time yourself carefully – and stop writing immediately your time is up. Don't refer to notes or books while you are writing.

Sections 5 and 6 of this book include some suggestions about how you might tackle the different types of questions you are likely to come across in the exam.

5 If you are one of the small number of students who gets so worried about exams that you are likely to *panic* on the actual day, you will need to work out in advance ways of helping yourself to cope. Think about what triggers off the panic. Perhaps it's the sight of other people writing and writing and writing. Perhaps it's other people going out for extra sheets of paper. Perhaps it's the memory of some earlier occasion when you panicked. Perhaps it's the fear of disappointing relatives who are desperately hoping you will do well. Just thinking about the cause can help you feel more able to cope with the feelings.

Talk about it with someone who is sympathetic (most people are - they've probably experienced something similar at some time in their lives). Some people find it helps to get themselves into a very relaxed state (e.g. lying down, eyes closed, thinking about some very peaceful scene) and then imagine doing all the things that are liable to cause panic (e.g. walking into the exam room, opening the question paper, beginning to write, noticing the other candidates sitting in front of them, watching the clock, etc.). If you are able to do all these things without panicking in imagination, it can help you do the same things without panicking on the actual day. Some people panic simply because they are badly prepared: they haven't done enough revision, they have forgotten how many questions they've got to answer, they arrive late for the exam, or they haven't brought a spare pen. These causes of panic are much easier to deal with - it's up to you to make sure they don't happen.

THE DAY BEFORE THE EXAM

Some of the day before the exam should be spent in last-minute revision. The summaries described earlier in this section will come in handy at this point, so read them through carefully. Read *all* your notes for topics you still don't feel too sure about. Look at any essay plans you have written in the course of your revision.

It is useful at this stage to remind yourself of exactly what you will have to do. Check that you know how long the paper is, how many sections it is divided into, how many questions you have to answer, and how long you will have for each of them. Where do you have to put your name, candidate number, centre number, etc.? What bits of the answer book are you *not* supposed to write on (e.g. margins)? Do you answer questions in spaces on the question paper or in a separate answer booklet? All this will be explained clearly in writing on the papers - but it's worth thinking about beforehand. The last thing you want at the beginning of an exam is to have to worry about where you are going to write your answers, what 'centre number' means and so on. Check also that you know what time the exam starts and where it is going to take place. Listen to the weather forecast for the next day and plan the clothes you will wear. Think about the exam room – are you likely to be sitting in the sunshine or is it always quite cool? There's nothing worse in an exam than feeling physically uncomfortable, and a bit of thought the day before can prevent this happening.

Check also that you have two pens, two pencils, a ruler and a rubber.

When you have done all these things, have a rest. Think about something else – and make sure you have a good night's sleep.

THE DAY OF THE EXAM

If you have done all the things suggested up to now, you will have little to worry about on the actual day. There are a few things, though, that are worth remembering.

1 Arrive at the exam room in plenty of time. Therefore get up in plenty of time, catch the bus in plenty of time, and so on.

2 Check again that you have pens, pencils, ruler etc., as needed.

3 Go to the loo before entering the exam room. If you need to go during the exam, just ask the person who is invigilating (supervising) the exam. Don't hesitate if you really need to go!

4 Make sure your desk isn't wobbly. This can be very irritating. If it is wobbly, ask the invigilator to put a wedge under the leg that's too short.

5 Read the rubric (i.e. instructions at the beginning of the question paper) very carefully. If you are asked to answer four questions, don't answer three or five. Do as the exam paper tells you.

6 Where you have a choice of questions, choose carefully, i.e. read them all through first. People often choose one question and start answering it, then realise that they actually know a lot more about another one, cross it all out and start again. Try to avoid that happening – it's a terrible waste of time.

7 Read all questions very carefully and make sure everything in your answer is relevant to the question you have been asked. If it isn't helping to answer that question, then don't put it down, because you won't get any marks for it, even if it is correct and well-written.

8 Number all your answers, e.g. *13, 14(a), 15(b)(i)*, etc. This is very important – otherwise the examiners won't know which question you're answering.

9 Pace yourself so that you don't run out of time at the end. If you find you are spending far too much time on, say, Section 1, bring your answer to a conclusion and move on to Section 2 (assuming of course that you know a lot about Section 2 as well).

10 If you run out of time, summarise the main points you intended to make. Do this in the form of an essay plan, like the one on pages 35–6.

Avoid having to do this if you can - notes don't usually score many marks - but it's better than nothing.

11 If you manage to finish before the end of the exam, don't just sit there and stare out of the window. Re-read what you have written. Even if you feel you have made a mess of things, there's always some amendment you can make that will improve your chances. Use every minute that is available to you.

12 Make sure you haven't missed out any parts of the questions you have chosen (or are told to answer). Some candidates lose a lot of marks simply by failing to turn over a page. Check this kind of thing very carefully.

13 Don't get worried about other people going out for more and more extra sheets of paper, even if you find you don't need any yourself. Sometimes the best answers are the briefest and the worst are the lengthiest. If you have revised thoroughly and write concisely, you should have nothing to worry about.

14 Don't worry if you have to cross things out. Examiners don't take this kind of thing into account when they are marking - unless it is so untidy that it becomes almost impossible to read. Some candidates get neurotic about this, removing every little blemish with large dollops of correcting fluid. This is a sheer waste of time. There are much more important things to be thinking about - above all, how best to tackle the different types of questions on the exam paper. This is what sections 5 and 6 will now help you to do.

SECTION 5

How to tackle short-answer questions and essays

GCSE History exams usually include four main types of questions. These are:

- **(a)** short-answer questions;
- **(b)** essay questions;
- **(c)** evidence questions;
- **(d)** stimulus questions.

One of the best ways of making sure you do well in your exam is to think about the skills you will need to tackle each type of question. This section looks at short-answer questions and essays. Section 6 explains evidence and stimulus questions.

SHORT-ANSWER QUESTIONS

One-word answer questions

Let's look first at the answers which require least writing. You might wonder what skills you need for one-word answer questions, such as this:

Name the politician whose election in British Guiana in the 1950s was viewed with suspicion by the British authorities.

Either you know it or you don't, you might say. You'd be right of course, but it isn't quite as simple as it seems. There were two major political leaders who were elected at different times in British Guiana during the 1950s: Forbes Burnham and Cheddi Jagan. Burnham was a moderate; Jagan was rumoured to have communist sympathies. It was Jagan therefore, not Burnham, who was *viewed with suspicion by the British authorities*. It would be easy to see '. . . politician . . . British

Guiana . . . 1950s', remember the name Forbes Burnham, and put that down as your answer without thinking any further. A lot of people would do that, and keep on doing it in other questions as well. Make sure you aren't one of them.

SUMMARY

In one-word answer questions:

Do *read the question carefully.*
Don't *put down the first answer that comes into your head.*
Do *stop to think.*
Do *give your memory time to work.*

Multiple choice questions

Another kind of short-answer question used by some exam boards is the multiple choice question. This is an example from a LEAG specimen paper:

Place a bold tick against the correct description of the trend of Jewish immigration into Palestine in the early 1930s.

Decreasing, because of American obstruction
Increasing, because of British encouragement
Decreasing, because of Jewish emigration
Increasing, because of German persecution
Decreasing, because of Arab opposition

As you can see, there are five possible answers or options, only one of which is correct. You put a tick or mark against the correct answer (or, in some exams, write down the answer in an answer book). Sometimes you will look at one of these questions and immediately spot what you think is the answer. You just *know* this is what happened. It's still a good idea to read the other four options with care, rejecting each one in turn, in order to check that you really did get it right. At other times you'll look at a question and none of the options will stand out as the obvious answer. It can even be a bit overwhelming, trying to keep all the parts of the question in your head at the same time. *Don't* panic. Read the question again, fixing all the key words in your mind: '. . . Jewish . . . Palestine . . . early 1930s'. Then take the options one by one. The first option you should be able to reject straight away. The second part of it may well sound convincing, but you know that Jewish immigration was increasing, *not* decreasing. This, then, eliminates the third and the fifth options as well, so you can concentrate on the second and the fourth. The second can't be right, because you know the British tried to *restrict* the number of Jews entering Palestine. That leaves the fourth: yes, Jewish immigration was increasing (you had established that already), yes (now you think about it!), this was largely because of Jews fleeing from Nazi persecution in Germany. You have got the right answer by eliminating all the wrong ones. If you tackle these multiple choice questions in a systematic way, you will feel more in control of what you are doing. Because of this you will make fewer careless mistakes.

SUMMARY

In multiple choice questions:

Don't *place your tick before reading all the options.*
Do *remember all the key words in the question.*
And *when you are not sure of the answer,* do *try to eliminate wrong answers one by one.*

'Write a sentence' questions

A third kind of short-answer question is when you are asked to write a sentence or couple of sentences about a topic. Here is an example from a Social and Economic History exam paper:

Write a sentence to explain the importance of Miss Buss and Miss Beale.
(2 marks)

and another from an exam paper on the Tudor and Stuart period:

Give *two* reasons why Charles I was executed. *(2 marks)*

You might be able to write a whole essay on either of these topics, but don't try to do so. The first question says: 'Write a sentence'. This has to be fitted into the two lines provided in the answer book. Candidates who continue their answers up and down the margins until the page begins to look like some medieval manuscript are not popular with examiners! Concentrate therefore on what is important. An answer to the first question might be:

> They were supporters of better education for girls and founded new girls' schools in the mid-nineteenth century.

This would easily get the 2 marks available for that question. There is no need to give the names and dates of the schools they founded, even if you knew them – which you probably wouldn't. On the other hand, don't be too vague: an answer that read 'They were important in nineteenth-century education' would get no marks.

Here are three answers to the question on Charles I. How many marks (out of 2) do you think each of them would get?

(a) Charles I was executed because he was an unsuccessful king who ruled badly.

(b) Charles I was executed because Parliament couldn't trust him and knew he would keep on trying to recover his power.

(c) Charles I was executed because his forces kept on being defeated by the New Model Army. Parliament believed that if he were allowed to live he would always be trying to take away their power.

Now check your marks with the ones an examiner gave them. Answer (a) got no marks. It is so vague and general that it really tells us nothing about why Charles I was executed. Lots of kings have ruled badly, but they didn't all end up being executed! Answer (b) got 1 mark. It gives a good general reason for Charles I's execution, but only one reason when the question asks for *two* (being convinced that the king will keep on trying to recover his power is the same thing as not trusting him). Answer (c) got the full 2 marks. It gives *two* reasons, which are clearly stated and clearly different from each other.

SUMMARY

In 'write a sentence' questions:

Don't *write more than you are asked to do.*
Do *concentrate on what is important (forget about the incidental details).*
Do *make your points clear and precise.*

'Fill in the gap' questions

Another type of short-answer question asks you to fill in the gaps in a sentence or paragraph. Here are two examples:

1 In each of the following questions choose the word, place, date or number that will make the sentence read accurately. Write your answers in the spaces (. . . . .) provided.

(a) By the Treaty of Berlin (1878) Britain obtained a protectorate over the island of . . . .

(b) . . . . was the German Chancellor who signed the Treaty of Berlin (1878).

(c) Shortly after the signing of the Treaty of Berlin Germany signed a treaty of defensive . . . . with . . . . . .

2 Read the following passage carefully. In the answer book provided, write down against each answer number, *1–7*, the word, phrase, or date which will make the passage read accurately and sensibly.

Chile and Argentina in the 1970s and early 1980s
During the years 1970–73 Chile was ruled by a Marxist President, Salvador . . . . . . *(1)*. In 1973 this President was overthrown by a . . . . . . *(2)* coup.

A similar coup took place in Argentina in . . . . . . *(3)*.
In the early 1980s Argentina became involved in a war with . . . . . .
(4) over the possession of the . . . . . . *(5)*.
This war ended in Argentina's . . . . *(6)* and led to the establishment of a new . . . . *(7)* government in that country.

Notice that sometimes you have to write your answer in the spaces provided and sometimes in a separate answer booklet. If you are writing in a booklet, take care to number all your answers clearly. In answering questions like these, read the passage carefully. When you have thought of the words that seem to fit, write them down, then read the whole passage again, double-checking that it is accurate and makes sense. Someone who wrote 'dictator' for *(7)* in Question *2* would not just be wrong – they would also be writing nonsense. You may not be too sure whether you have got the right answer, but you can at least avoid completing the sentence in such a way that it fails to read sensibly.

SUMMARY

In 'fill in the gap' questions:

Do *read the passage a number of times.*
Do *check that your answers make sense.*
Don't *forget to number your answers.*

Some GCSE papers also include short-answer questions that are based on a picture or a short written source. These are known as *stimulus questions*. You can find examples of these questions in section 6.

ESSAY QUESTIONS

Structured questions

In the past, many history exam papers consisted of nothing but essay questions. They are still a very important part of most GCSE History exams. In answering them you stand to gain (or lose) a lot of marks. Most essay questions are what are called *structured* questions. This means that the topic is divided up (or structured) into various parts as a way of guiding you through it. Your answer must follow this structure step by step. For example:

(a) Outline the development of the Nazi Party in Germany during the 1920s.
(b) Show how the Nazi Party increased its power in Germany in the early 1930s.
(c) Why were so many Germans willing to support the Nazi Party at this time?

The question is about the rise to power of the Nazis, but it does *not* ask you to write all you know about Hitler and the Nazi Party. In part *(a)*, notice the word 'outline'. This means 'describe' or 'give an account of'; it is asking you to tell the story of the Nazi Party during the 1920s. It does not mean 'explain', so you are not being asked to look at the deep-rooted reasons why Nazism became important. Notice also the word 'development'. This is asking you to concentrate on how the party changed and expanded, not on how it was organised at a particular time. In part *(b)*, notice the words 'show how' and 'increased'. As in *(a)*, examiners are not asking about deep-rooted causes. Nor do they want you to write about any of the Nazi setbacks of those years. (Look again at that word 'increased'.) Save your explanation for part *(c)* where 'why' asks for reasons and nothing else.

If you pay attention to the different things the question is asking you to do (assuming of course that you know the topic), you shouldn't go far wrong. So always spend a couple of minutes reading and re-reading the question before you begin to write. Some people find it helps to underline, on the question paper, key words like *development*, *increased* and *why*, as a way of fixing them in their minds. Practise doing this with the following questions. Write them out in full and then underline the words that tell you how the topic has to be tackled.

1 *(a)* Explain now the Younger Pitt, from being a newly elected MP in 1781, became Prime Minister in 1783.
   (b) Give an account of Pitt's achievements as peacetime Prime Minister during the years 1783–93.
   (c) How far and for what reasons do you agree that the Younger Pitt was an unsuccessful war minister?

2 *(a)* What is the meaning of *free trade*?
   (b) Give *two* arguments, used in the nineteenth century, in favour of free trade, and *two* arguments against.
   (c) Describe the part played by *one* of the following in the development of free trade:
      (i) Pitt
      (ii) Huskisson
      (iii) Gladstone

3 *(a)* What did the Chartists demand?
   (b) What were the reasons for the rise of the Chartist movement?
   (c) Why did the Chartists fail?
   (d) To what extent would you agree that the Chartists were a 'complete failure'?

4 *(a)* Trace the steps during the 1920s that led to the calling of a General Strike in Britain in 1926.

(b) Describe the events of the General Strike, showing how it came to an end.

(c) Why has the General Strike been considered an important episode in British history?

5 Explain and assess the significance of the establishment of each of the following mutual defence alliances:

(a) NATO
(b) Warsaw Pact
(c) SEATO
(d) CENTO

When you have finished, look at this list of words often found in GCSE history questions:

Outline the events that led to . . .	Describe how . . .
Explain why . . .	Account for . . .
Show the importance of . . .	Show how far . . .
Give an account of . . .	For what reasons did . . .?
Why did . . .?	How did . . .?
Assess . . .	Trace the . . .
To what extent did . . .?	Show in what ways . . .

Think about what each of these is telling you to do. Make sure you understand how they differ from each other. Most of them fall into two main types: 'describe' questions, which ask for an account or description; and 'explain' questions, which ask for reasons or explanations. 'Describe' questions include 'Outline the events . . . ', 'Give an account of . . . ', 'Describe how . . . ', 'How did . . . ?', 'Show in what ways . . . ' and 'Trace the . . . '. 'Explain' questions include 'Explain why . . . ', 'For what reasons did . . . ?', and 'Why did . . . ?' Notice the difference between 'give an account of' and 'account for'. They look similar, but are actually asking for quite different things – the first to tell the story, the second to explain. 'Show how far . . .' and 'To what extent did . . .?' are also different, in that they ask you to assess as well as to describe or explain. You might be asked, for example, to discuss 'how far' or 'to what extent' Germany was responsible for the outbreak of the First World War. This involves looking at both the ways in which Germany was responsible and the ways in which it was not, and then saying which you think were the more important.

Once you are clear about the instructions in a question, the next step is to jot down a brief *plan* of the main points you want to make. Do this in the way suggested in section 4. Then begin to write, but keep on looking back at the question – just to check that you aren't being sidetracked.

Sample answers

On the next few pages, you will find two answers to the question about the Nazis on page 44. In both answers you will be able to see how many marks were obtained. They are marked out of 20, with 6/7 marks for each of parts *(a)*, *(b)* and *(c)*. The first answer only received 6 marks altogether. As you read it, try to think why that was.

Germany lost a lot of land at the end of the First World War. Many Germans were fed up with the Treaty of Versailles. There was a lot of violence and the currency was almost worthless. People used to take home their wages in wheelbarrows. A lot lost all their savings. Hitler was sick of all this and founded a new party to put Germany back on its feet. But he got arrested and wrote *Mein Kampf* in prison. Then he founded the SA and the SS, but didn't get much support because things got more prosperous after 1924. Then came the Wall Street Crash and inflation started up all over again. Hitler won more seats in parliament. Hindenburg the President was an old man and Hitler was able to persuade him to make him Chancellor. This happened in 1934. Hitler had got rid of the Communists because of the Reichstag fire. This gave him the excuse to lock many of them up. Therefore he won the election and persuaded the parliament to give him power as a dictator. He then began to turn against the Jews and in 1935 there was a terrible pogrom all over Germany. Many Jews were beaten up and sent to concentration camps. Germans supported Hitler because he said he was going to solve Germany's economic problems. He was also a good speaker. He won people over to his side. The SA were very brutal and beat up opponents. Many Germans hadn't a clue what they were letting themselves in for. They thought it was going to be very different from what actually happened when he came to power.

There are some good points here and there – especially perhaps in the last few sentences. Overall, however, it's a weak answer. Try to think *why* it wasn't very successful. These are the kind of reasons you should come up with:

1 It is too short. There is a lot more that might be said about such an important topic. There are 20 marks for this question and 35 minutes in which to answer it.

2 It isn't always clear which part of the question is being answered. Where does part *(a)* end and part *(b)* begin? The last five sentences seem to refer to part *(c)*, but it would have helped to have started a new paragraph at that point and to have put *(c)* at the beginning of this paragraph to make it quite clear which bit of the question was being answered.

3 There are a number of factual errors, e.g. inflation did not start up again after the Wall Street Crash, Hitler became Chancellor in 1933, not 1934, etc.

4 Quite a lot of comments are irrelevant, because they don't answer the question. Part *(a)* asks you to outline the development of the Nazi Party. The first five sentences don't refer to this directly at all. Later on there are two sentences about Hitler's attacks on the Jews in the mid-1930s. Again this isn't relevant to part *(b)*, which asks about how the Nazi Party increased its power in the *early* 1930s.

5 Some comments are very vague, e.g. 'He won people over to his side.' This is so obvious it isn't worth saying. In fact it is already given in the question. What the answer should be doing is showing *why* Hitler was able to do this.

6 The various points, even when relevant, don't seem to follow any clear kind of order. They seem almost to be flung down at random. There is no sign that the answer has been carefully planned.

7 There are no paragraphs.

8 Some of the language is a bit sloppy, e.g. 'were fed up', 'was sick of all this', 'hadn't a clue'. It isn't the kind of cautious and precise language that historians use.

The second answer to the same question obtained almost full marks. It manages to avoid all the problems we found in the first answer.

(a) The Nazi Party was founded in 1919. At first it was a very small organisation, confined to Bavaria in southern Germany. It was one of many extreme right-wing organisations that sprang up during the period immediately after the end of the First World War. Associated with it was a semi-military organisation, controlled by Ernst Röhm, known as the SA or brownshirts. The programme of the Nazi Party was both nationalist and socialist. It was nationalist in that it was very concerned about making Germany once again the most powerful country in Europe. It was socialist in the sense that its progress included a lot of demands for social and economic reform. Its leader, Hitler, was much more interested in nationalist issues than in social ones. Many members of the SA, however, took the party's 'socialism' very seriously.

The party first became known outside Bavaria in 1923 when Hitler tried to seize power in Munich. This was known as the Munich putsch. The French were occupying the Ruhr at this time and Hitler hoped that Germans would turn to him as a strong leader who would save their country from further humiliation. The putsch, however, failed. Hitler spent some time in prison where he wrote *Mein Kampf*. This book became the bible of the Nazi Party. In it Hitler put down his ideas about Germany's greatness, about the superiority of the German race, and the need for strong government.

Hitler's trial received a great deal of publicity. As a result, more people learned about the Nazis and what they were trying to do. The failure of the putsch convinced Hitler that he would only come to power by means of elections. He therefore set about strengthening the party's organisation, setting up branches in different parts of Germany and creating another semi-military organisation known as the SS or blackshirts.

Although the Nazi Party was much better organised, it did not attract a great deal of support during the 1920s. This was mainly because of the economic prosperity of those years. The Wall Street Crash at the end of 1929 changed the situation overnight. Mass unemployment gave Hitler the chance to put himself forward as the man who was going to solve all Germany's problems.

(b) Because of the Wall Street Crash, the Nazi Party increased its support in the Reichstag election of 1930. Some businessmen now began to give financial support to the party. Hitler also won the backing of some leading newspaper owners who were able to improve the party's publicity. Branches of the party were formed in parts of Germany where it had previously been almost unknown. In 1932 Hitler stood as a candidate in the presidential election. Although beaten by Hindenburg, Hitler won 13 million votes (to Hindenburg's 19 million).

In July 1932 there were also elections for the Reichstag. The Nazis were very successful in these elections, becoming the largest single party in the Reichstag. The Chancellor, Von Papen, found it almost impossible to govern without Hitler's support. Hitler, however, was determined not to accept office under anyone else. In November 1932 a second election was held. The Nazis got fewer seats, but were still the largest single party. A new Chancellor, Von Schleicher, was appointed, but he found it just as difficult to govern. Hindenburg eventually agreed to appoint Hitler as Chancellor in January 1933. He was to be head of a coalition government.

To Hitler this was just a first step to complete power. His aim was to obtain an Enabling Act that would give him the power to rule as a dictator. He arrested many Communists, accusing them unjustly of being responsible for a fire that burnt down the Reichstag building. New Reichstag elections were held in March 1933. During the elections the SA used a lot of violence against other parties. Despite this the Nazis received less than half of the seats. With support from the right-wing Nationalists and from the Centre Party (to whom he made all sorts of promises), Hitler however got his Enabling Act. Soon the Nazi Party was the only one allowed. The Third Reich had begun.

(c) Many Germans were willing to support the Nazis at this time for a number of reasons. The Weimar leaders of the early 1930s seemed powerless to stop Germany's economic decline. The Nazis won support because they looked as if they might provide the strong government that would enable Germany to recover. Many Germans were very nationalistic and Hitler's talk about Germany's greatness was especially popular.

Some Germans were also worried about the Communists, who also grew stronger after 1929. Hitler looked as if he would be able to deal with them more effectively than democratic politicians. Many middle-class people particularly feared what would happen to their wealth if the Communists came to power.

Hitler was also able to win support because he was such a good orator. He organised impressive rallies at which he whipped up people's feelings. His talk about the Jews also gave people a scapegoat for all their problems.

Some Germans also did not know what they were letting themselves in for. They were attracted by Hitler's energy and enthusiasm, but ignored those bits of his programme that they didn't like. In a way they allowed themselves to be deceived.

This is only one of a number of ways in which this question might be tackled. There are a lot of other reasons, for example, that might have been included in answer *(c)*. It would be very difficult, however, to do much better in the time available. In order to help you understand why this answer obtained high marks when the other one didn't, go through all the criticisms of the first answer and see how they *don't* apply in this case. Notice especially how the second answer is well-structured, how the information it contains is precise, and how every sentence is related to this particular question.

SUMMARY

In structured essay questions:

Don't *include material that isn't asked for.*
Do *show how your points relate to the question. (Look again at the third part of the second answer.)*
Do *write precisely.*
Do *organise your answer into different sections.*
Do *use paragraphs.*

Other structured essay questions

These questions are really very similar to the ones you have been looking at so far – though they might seem different at first glance. Here is
one example:

**Explain why there was so much support for the Chartists in the 1830s
and 1840s. Make use of each of the following:**
    the campaign against the New Poor Law
    the factory reform movement
    economic developments in 1839, 1842 and 1848
    revolutions in Europe
    Chartist newspapers and pamphlets
    working and living conditions
    discontent with the parliamentary system

The question is trying to help you by suggesting some of the main parts
into which your answer might be divided. You may wish to put some of
the headings together, e.g. economic developments and working and
living conditions. You may even think of reasons for Chartist support
that aren't covered by any of the headings. You must include some
comments, however, on each of the topics that are listed. Remember
that this is still an essay. Don't present your answer as a series of notes
on each of the topics in turn. Use sub-headings only if the question
specifically asks you to do so, as in this example:

**Write an account of the history of Canada during the years since 1945,
making use of the following headings: *(a)* economic developments; *(b)*
the problem of regional separatism; *(c)* relations with other states.**

In this case, write out each heading before you begin to answer that
part of the question.

Empathy questions

This type of essay question is rather different. These questions test the
empathy that you read about in section 2. Here are a few examples:

1 *(a)* **Imagine you are a leading member of the factory reform movement during the late 1830s. Write a letter to a newspaper
explaining why you think that a further measure of factory
reform is necessary.** *(10 marks)*

    (b) **Imagine you are an opponent of the factory reform movement
during the early 1840s. Write a letter to the Home Secretary
opposing government plans for a further measure of factory
reform.** *(10 marks)*

2 **Imagine you are a South Wales miner who took part in the General
Strike of 1926. Write your memoirs for this period in your life,**

describing why you became involved in the General Strike and what
happened to you. *(20 marks)*

3 You are an immigrant from *either* the West Indies *or* the Indian subcontinent who has arrived in Britain during the early 1960s. Explain
why you decided to come to Britain and describe your experiences
there during the first few years after your arrival. *(20 marks)*

As you can see, these questions are asking you to put yourself in the
position of someone in the past. You have got to imagine yourself as that
person and write as that person might have written. This usually means
saying things like 'I think this . . . ', 'I did that . . . ', 'My purpose in
writing this letter is to . . . '. An answer to *1(a)* that read 'Factory
reformers usually felt that it was cruel to employ young children for
long hours . . . ' would have failed to display the imagination that the
question requires, and would be unlikely to get many marks.

In questions like these, you will already know a lot about the topic,
e.g. factory reform or the General Strike. You will have to use this
knowledge to help you imagine what it would have been like to take
part in these events. Think about the feelings people might have had.
Think about the beliefs they would have held. Think also about how
they would have expressed themselves when writing about their experiences. This involves taking into account the way the question asks you
to write your answer. A letter to a newspaper *(1)* is written in a different
way from someone's memoirs *(2)*. Both of these, in their turn, are
different from a private letter or from a speech delivered in parliament.
You may be asked to write any of these. You should also take into
account the period in which you are supposed to be writing and the
person you are supposed to be. If you were an ambassador writing to a
king, you would be likely to address him differently from a member of
your family or a friend. If you were supposed to be writing in the
nineteenth century you would be unlikely to write such phrases as:

Gladstone seems really cheesed off with the Irish . . .
The British here think that Kruger is a crazy guy . . .

(Both of these are taken from students' answers.) You are not expected
to imitate the way in which Victorians would have written, because you
probably won't know enough about them to do that. But you can at
least avoid expressions that sound hopelessly wrong for the period.

If you really make the effort to imagine how these people would
have felt and thought, you won't be capable of answering these questions in the kind of vague and general way that usually ends up with
very low marks. This is the sort of answer to *1(a)* that you should *not*
be writing:

Dear Sir,

I think conditions in factories are absolutely disgusting. They are a disgrace to the country and something should be done about them as soon as possible. It's terrible what is happening to people who work in these factories. I think the government should step in and make some reforms. There's no time to lose.

Yours faithfully,
A. Rawlinson

This is so vague and general it could apply just as well to the USA in the 1890s, Nigeria in the 1960s, or South Korea in the 1970s.

A good answer to the same question is given below. It is precise and accurate. It shows an understanding of someone else's point of view, and is written in the way in which a letter to a newspaper might be written.

Thirstin Mill,
Honley
3 February 1839

Dear Sir,

Your readers will have learnt from the article in today's *Express* that the Whig government has decided against introducing a further measure of factory reform. Once again I feel compelled to draw to the attention of your readers the many reasons why such a measure is long overdue.

Firstly, as most of your readers are well aware, the conditions of many children and young persons working in factories is a disgrace to a civilised nation. They work long hours for very little pay. They have little or no time in which to learn their lessons. Many are too exhausted on the Sabbath to attend chapel. Some have become physically ill – even deformed – as a result of their labours. The worst conditions are now less common than they were – the 1833 Factory Act has at least achieved that. Yet everyone knows how often that Act is ignored. How could it be otherwise when there are only a handful of inspectors to deal with all the factories in the country! What we need now is a greater restriction on hours and more inspectors to make sure that this restriction is enforced.

Our main concern must be for the children, but we should not forget (secondly) about the adult workers in these mills. Child labour allows many factory owners to keep their mills running 15 or 16 hours a day. Adult workers are forced to work these excessive hours if they wish to remain in employment. Restrict the hours of children and young persons and you will in effect restrict the hours of adult workers as well. If they are more contented, these workers will be less likely to give their support to those dangerous Chartist ideas currently circulating among discontented persons in the neighbourhood.

As most of your readers will know, I am, Sir, one of the leading factory owners in this district. I have long restricted the hours of my workers to a maximum of ten. In no way have I suffered by doing so. Not only are my workers healthier, harder working and more respectful, but my own profits have even increased. I can recommend such a system to all other factory owners – and to the government – on the grounds both of common sense and of humanity.

> I remain, Sir, your obedient servant,
> Josiah Hopkinson

The Editor,
The Holme Valley Express

Notice one other feature of this answer: it shows that the person writing it realises how difficult it is to generalise about the views of whole groups of people in the past. Most factory owners probably opposed factory reform. Some, however, didn't. This *variety* of opinions comes across very clearly. Students who have understood this have obviously succeeded in imagining themselves back into the past. They have grasped that these were real people (with all their differences), not just cardboard figures in some history text-book.

Empathy questions require a lot of practice. They are among the most difficult questions you will have to tackle, but they can also be the most enjoyable to answer.

SUMMARY

In empathy questions:

Do *alter your writing according to the form it is supposed to take (e.g. a letter, or memoirs).*
Do *write as if you were the person you are supposed to be.*
Do *include a lot of precise and relevant detail.*
Don't *give the impression that everyone thought or felt the same.*
Do *try to be interesting and lively. The best empathy answers are enjoyable to read.*

SECTION 6

How to tackle evidence and stimulus questions

EVIDENCE QUESTIONS

All GCSE History exams will include questions testing those skills in handling evidence that you read about in section 2 (see pages 16 to 22). In most GCSE History exams, quite a high proportion of the marks are likely to be awarded for these evidence questions, so it is particularly important that you have some practice in handling them.

The evidence on which questions are based will be of different kinds. There will be some written sources (e.g. letters, diaries, newspapers, reports, Acts of Parliament, extracts from treaties) and some visual sources (e.g. photographs, posters, cartoons, pictures). There may also be maps. Some sources may be primary sources for the period that you are studying; others may be secondary sources (see page 16). Whatever the source, you will need to read it and/or look at it very closely before you begin to answer the questions. If you are given more than one source to study at a time, this may be quite a lengthy business. Don't rush it. The more you understand what the sources are about, the better – and the faster – you will be able to answer the questions that follow. In Paper 2 of the exam for the Schools History Project, you are likely to be given fifteen minutes reading time before you begin to answer the question. Make sure you use it.

There are many different types of evidence-based questions. Before looking at these types in turn, there are a number of general points that you will need to bear in mind. Let's examine a particular set of questions based on an early nineteenth-century report:

Study this account of a meeting held at Hunslet Moor in 1819, and then answer questions *(a)* to *(e)* which follow.

Two caps of Liberty next passed, one of which was profusely adorned with various-coloured ribands, and round the other the word *Liberty* was printed . . . On another flag was inscribed *We demand our rights as* men. *Liberty, Justice and Humanity.* One of the most remarkable and appropriate flags bore the device of a man in irons, with a padlock in his mouth, and his pockets turned inside out, bending under two immense burdens of *National Debt* and *Taxation*. At the top was written *A Free-Born Englishman*; and at the bottom *Britons Never Shall Be Slaves*. Another flag bore the inscription *Hunt and Liberty. No Corn Laws.* Another expressed the grand wish of the Radical Reformers in the words *Annual Parliaments, Universal Suffrage, and Vote by Ballot* . . .

ribands: ribbons
bore the device: had a drawing on it

(a) Explain in your own words what is meant by
  (i) *National Debt*   *(2 marks)*
  (ii) *Corn Laws*   *(2 marks)*
  (iii) *Universal Suffrage*   *(2 marks)*
(b) Quote one phrase from this source that is expressing an *opinion* rather than just stating a *fact*.   *(2 marks)*
(c) Does this piece of evidence prove that most radical reformers demanded *Universal Suffrage*? Give reasons for your answer.
                                                       (3 marks)
(d) Using both the source and your own knowledge, explain why one of the flags had on it the drawing described in lines 5–7 of the extract.   *(8 marks)*
(e) You are a historian studying popular protest movements during the years 1815–20.
  (i) What problems would you face in using this source? *(3 marks)*
  (ii) What might be the value of this source?   *(3 marks)*

General points

1 Pay close attention to the *number of marks* allocated to each part of the question. These are printed on the exam paper as a way of showing how much time you ought to be spending on each part. You can expect to spend more time on part *(d)*, to which 8 marks have been allocated, than on part *(b)* which only receives 2 marks. If you find you are writing as much on *(b)* as you are on *(d)*, you are likely to be doing one of two things: *either* failing to answer *(d)* as fully as you should *or* spending an unnecessarily long time on *(b)*. Sometimes you can answer high-scoring questions well by writing very little. It's much safer, however, to assume that usually you can't. (In some papers you will have to write your answers in the spaces that have been provided for you in the exam booklet. This gives you a further guide to the amount of time you should be spending on each question.)

When tackling a sub-question like *(d)*, which has a high mark allocation, it might be helpful, as in essay questions, to jot down a brief plan of the main points you want to make. A plan for part *(d)* might be something like this:

> *Man in irons*: shows belief of reformers that people didn't have liberty (e.g. no ballot/univ. suffrage etc.). Own knowledge: habeas corpus suspended/repression of protests (e.g. Peterloo).
> *Padlock in mouth*: idea of liberty again. Own knowledge: restrictions on press & meetings.
> *Empty pockets/burdens*: general idea of oppressive govt. Own knowledge: probably refers to indirect taxes (income tax abolished in 1816).

You may be able to keep all this in your head – in which case it would be a waste of time to make a plan. On the other hand, it might be very helpful – and might save you time.

2 *Read* the questions carefully. As in essay questions, notice (and underline) key words, such as *explain* in part *(d)* and *prove* in part *(c)*. These words have been chosen with great care and mean precisely what they say, i.e. *explain* does *not* mean 'describe', *prove* does *not* mean 'suggest' or 'imply'. In answering the questions, do precisely what these instruction words tell you to do. In *(c)*, for example, you might feel that this evidence *suggests* that most radical reformers demanded universal suffrage. The writer of the report certainly seems to think that they did. (Look at the phrase 'the grand wish of the Radical Reformers' in the last sentence.) That wouldn't be the point, though. The question asks whether the evidence *proves* that they demanded universal suffrage. The answer of course is that it doesn't. We don't know who the writer of the report was. He might not have been in a position to know what most radical reformers were demanding. He might, on the other hand, have been in a position to know, but might have had reasons for concealing the truth from his readers. He might even have reported inaccurately what was written on this particular flag. In other words we most certainly don't have *proof* – and that was all the question was asking you to comment on. You might scrape a few marks even if your answer doesn't focus on the word *prove*, but you certainly wouldn't get full marks.

Notice especially where words are used in the singular and where they are used in the plural. If a question asks for reason*s* as in *(c)*, one reason isn't going to be enough. If it asks for problem*s*, as in *(e)*(i), again one problem isn't going to be adequate.

Some questions require an answer that is both taken from the evidence itself *and* from your own knowledge. This is what part *(d)* is asking for. In order to answer the question, you have to do both. If you don't, you are unlikely to get more than half marks (if that). It can be very tempting in a question like this to forget about the sources and just put down all the things you know about repressive Toryism during the years 1815–19. Resist the temptation. Look carefully at the plan (p. 57) for *(d)*. Notice how it comments on each part of the drawing on the flag and how, in each part, it uses both the evidence in the passage *and* the candidate's own knowledge.

3 Where a question asks you to explain or describe or summarise something *in your own words*, make sure this is what you do. Answers that simply quote the passage are unlikely to receive any marks. In part *(a)* you are asked to explain the meaning of three important terms. The term in **(iii)** is *Universal Suffrage*. These are three possible answers to this question (with the mark – out of 2 – shown in brackets):

   (a) It means that people were to be given the suffrage.   *(0 marks)*
   (b) Universal suffrage means having the right to vote.   *(1 mark)*
   (c) It means that everyone was to have the right to vote in elections.
                                                               (2 marks)

Answer **(a)** doesn't explain the word *suffrage* in the candidate's own words, so the examiner doesn't know whether the candidate understands what it means or not. The reference to 'people' is also very vague: does this mean all people or some people? It isn't clear. There is nothing here even to show that the candidate knows what *universal* means. The answer therefore gets no marks. Answer **(b)** is obviously better. This candidate knows what *suffrage* means, but doesn't explain *universal*. The answer therefore cannot obtain full marks. Answer **(c)** does both things, i.e. explains both *universal* ('everyone') and *suffrage* ('the right to vote in elections') – and in the candidate's *own words*.

This is quite a straightforward example. Some questions might ask for something more demanding, e.g. to summarise the main points being made in a piece of evidence, and you might feel tempted to use the words that are already there. Try hard not to do so. Think how the writer of the passage makes the point and then work out a way of putting it in your own words. Suppose you were asked to 'describe in your own words the kinds of flags on display at the meeting'. You should try not to quote what the writer says, e.g. 'one flag bore the device of a man in irons . . . another expressed the grand wish of the Radical Reformers . . .'. Answer instead with sentences such as: 'The flags had inscriptions on them, demanding various rights and criticising some of the ways in which Britain was governed. There were a lot of references to freedom and liberty. One flag had a drawing as well as an inscription.' This would make all the main points about the flags – and do so in *your own words*.

4 There are some questions, on the other hand, which *ask you to quote* words from the passage. Part *(b)* is an example of this kind of question. You will only get your marks here if you do precisely as you

are asked, i.e. quote the exact words. You wouldn't get any marks, for example, for saying that the writer of the report thought one of the flags was 'very interesting'. That would not be quoting what he said. The main danger with this kind of question, however, is that you might quote too much, e.g. your quotation might (in this case) include both an expression of opinion and a statement of fact. For example: 'One of the most remarkable and appropriate flags bore the device of a man in irons.' The statement that a flag 'bore the device of a man in irons' is clearly a statement of fact, but the answer also expresses an opinion, i.e. that the flag was 'remarkable' etc. So this answer includes both fact and opinion, and is incorrect. Check very carefully that the words you quote only illustrate whatever you are trying to illustrate – and don't suggest other things that might be the opposite of the point you are trying to make.

5 *Number* your answers carefully, i.e. *(a)(i)*, *(a)(ii)*, *(b)*, etc., otherwise the examiner might not know which sub-question your answer refers to. It is also best to do these questions in the right order. Apart from helping the examiner, you will be helping yourself, because often later questions are easier once you have worked your way through the earlier ones. In this example, answering part *(a)* will make it easier for you to answer parts *(d)* and *(e)*.

SUMMARY

In evidence questions:

Do *notice how many marks are awarded to each question – and spend your time accordingly.*

Do *read the questions carefully, noting key words, plurals, etc.*

Don't *copy out the passage when you are asked to use your own words.*

Don't *quote more than you need to prove the particular point you are making (e.g. in fact–opinion questions).*

Do *number your answers.*

Do *answer in the right order.*

The main types of evidence questions

Most of the main types of evidence questions are illustrated in the example you have just been studying.

1 *Comprehension questions*

These are designed to test your understanding of the evidence as a whole and of certain words and ideas within it. Part *(a)* is an example of this kind of question. Remember that the evidence may also be visual. For example, you might be asked to describe the main point a cartoonist is trying to make, or explain what is happening in a painting.

2 *Questions asking you to test the evidence against a particular statement*

For example, a question might ask whether the evidence proves or suggests something. Part *(c)* is an example of this kind of question. Another example is this question from a LEAG Schools History paper:

(a) 'Tenochtitlan (Mexico City) was built on an island in a lake. There were three causeways, canals, wide streets and large temples.'

Which sources would you choose to support these statements? Give the reasons for your choice of Sources.   *(5 marks)*

(b) 'Tenochtitlan (Mexico City) amazed the Spanish, who were impressed by its size and beauty.'

Is there enough evidence in the Sources to support this statement? Give reasons for your answer.   *(5 marks)*

The sources here included four accounts of Tenochtitlan written in the sixteenth century, two sixteenth-century drawings, a photograph and a modern artist's reconstruction. Some of the sources support the statements in the questions; some of them don't. The skill here is in deciding which ones do, and showing how they do. Always check your statements against the evidence. Be cautious about the claims you make.

3 *Questions asking you to distinguish between fact and opinion*

These can be difficult. In searching a source for expressions of opinion, look out for words that make the writer's feelings clear, or show that he or she approves or disapproves of certain things. In the following passage, the opinions are in italics:

> The *justifiable* anger of the Third Estate found expression in the Tennis Court Oath. Their demands were still of a *very modest* kind, despite growing evidence of the King's hostility to any change that might weaken his power. Under the *able* leadership of . . .

If you are asked to identify a statement that is just a statement of fact, look for something that very clearly does not involve feelings or judgements about whether something is good or bad, e.g. 'Another flag bore the inscription *Hunt and Liberty*', 'The crown threw stones at the speaker . . . ', 'The Prime Minister introduced the Bill with a speech . . . '. Here is another example of this kind of question from a LEAG Schools History paper:

Read Source H. Select one example of a factual statement and one example of an opinion from this Source.   *(2 marks)*

Source H
These great towns and temples and buildings rising from the water all made of stone seemed like an enchanted vision . . . Indeed some of

60

our soldiers asked whether it was not all a dream . . . It was all so wonderful that I do not know how to describe this first glimpse of things never heard of, seen or dreamed of before. (We entered the city and went to the top of a temple.) So we stood looking about us, for that huge and cursed temple stood so high that from it we could see over everything very well, and we saw the three causeways . . . the fresh water . . . which supplies the city . . . and we beheld on that great lake a great multitude of canoes . . . and we saw temples and shrines like towers and fortresses all gleaming white, and it was a wonderful thing to behold . . . .

(Bernal Diaz's account, about 1576)

One mark is likely to be awarded for the factual statement and one mark for the opinion. There are many examples in this passage of both facts and opinions, so it is especially important to quote just the one you are trying to illustrate. A correct answer to this question might be:

One example of a factual statement is the sentence: 'We entered the city and went to the top of a temple.' One example of an opinion is the phrase 'It was all so wonderful'.

4 *Questions asking you to distinguish between primary and secondary sources*
These will also ask you to give reasons for the distinctions that you make. A simple question of this kind might ask whether the 1819 report you read earlier in this section was a primary or a secondary source and to give reasons for your answer. All you would need to say here would be: 'This report is a primary source for the study of early nineteenth-century Britain. It appears to have been written at the time to which it refers. The writer also seems to have been present at the meeting that he describes.'

Sometimes, however, it might not be quite so easy to decide what kind of source you are dealing with. Take this passage, for example:

Lord John Russell wrote to Edward Baines, editor of the *Leeds Mercury* and leader of local middle-class radicals, asking him about the effects of a £10 franchise in Leeds. The news that the working class would be largely excluded was reassuring. Baines obtained his information from thirty canvassers who had worked for the Liberals at the 1831 election.

. . . In the township of Holbeck, containing 11 000 inhabitants, chiefly of the working classes, but containing several mills, dye-houses, public houses, and respectable dwellings, there are only 150 voters . . . Out of 140 householders, heads of families, work-ing in the mill of Messrs Marshall and Co., there are *only two* who will have votes . . . Out of 160 or 170 householders in the mill of

Messrs O. Willans and Sons, Holbeck, there is *not one* vote. Out of about 100 householders in the employment of Messrs Taylor and Wordsworth, machine makers [the highest class of mechanics] *only one* has a vote. It appeared that of the working classes, not more than one in fifty would be enfranchised by the Bill . . .
(D.G. Wright, *Democracy and Reform 1815–1885*, 1970)

The book from which all of this is taken is a secondary source for the history of parliamentary reform in nineteenth-century Britain. It was written by a modern historian and published long after the events with which it is concerned. It contains, however, a lengthy quotation from what is obviously a primary source, i.e. a letter or report written by someone at the time. Both these points would need to be made.

5 Questions asking you to comment on the bias or reliability of particular sources

These may sometimes take the form of a request to comment on the writer's or cartoonist's *attitude* or *viewpoint*. The aim is to get you to write about the ways in which the writer or cartoonist looks at the event or situation he or she is describing. With written sources, this is often where your skills in distinguishing between fact and opinion will come in very useful. Read once again the brief passage about the Third Estate on page 60. The writer's attitude or viewpoint here is favourable to the Third Estate, i.e. he seems to be biased in favour of that group of people. This might make you cautious about accepting too readily what he says. His *bias* might have made him *unreliable*, e.g. in selecting material that shows the Third Estate in a good light and the King in a bad light. If asked to comment on his attitude/bias/reliability, these are the points you might make. If you were asked to back up these points with direct reference to the passage, you would need to quote the words 'justifiable', 'very modest' and 'able', all of which suggest the writer's favourable opinion of one particular group of French people in 1789.

In answering questions such as this, always try to make your points as precisely as possible, e.g. (on a passage about Mensheviks and Bolsheviks in Russia) 'The writer comments favourably on both the Mensheviks and the Bolsheviks, but has fewer criticisms to make of the latter group', rather than 'The writer is pro-Bolshevik.' The second statement might be a good general comment on the passage to which it refers, but the first statement is more precise and (if correct) is a much better answer.

Some questions might also ask how you would check the accuracy or reliability of a source. Points you might make here would include finding out more about the author and his or her attitudes, and checking this account against others that date from the same period.

6 *Questions about the problems that particular sources might cause the historian*

These are closely linked to the previous group of questions. Here is one example:

What are the disadvantages for a historian studying Britain during the first half of the nineteenth century of

(a) **contemporary drawings (as in Source A),**
(b) **newspaper articles (as in Source B), and**
(c) **government reports (as in Source C)?**

Let's look at *(c)*, which – like the other two parts – was allocated 4 marks. This is what Source C says:

> *Margaret Leveston*, 6 years old, coal-bearer in the East of Scotland coalfield; described by Mr Franks, the Sub-Commissioner, as 'a most interesting child, and perfectly beautiful'. She said: 'Been down at coal-carrying six weeks; makes ten to fourteen rakes [journeys] a day; carries full 56 lbs of coal in a wooden backit [Scots for a shallow wooden trough]. The work is na guid; it is so very sair. I work with sister Jesse and mother; dinna ken the time we gang; it is gai dark.'
> *(Parliamentary Papers*, 1842, from the Report of the Commission inquiring into the state of children in mines)

This is the kind of answer to *(c)* that ought to get full marks:

> The disadvantage of this kind of source is that the people writing it might only include evidence that backs up their own point of view. The Commissioners might be trying to give the impression that conditions in mines were worse than they really were. This particular girl's experience *might* be very untypical. We also do not know if witnesses are being quoted accurately. Another disadvantage might be the girl's age. A six year old might not be very reliable, e.g. about how many pounds of coal she carries.

Notice how the answer mentions more than one disadvantage. Notice also how it makes *general* points about government reports, but relates these to *specific* features of this particular extract. Nineteenth-century government reports of course have many advantages as well as disadvantages. The answer, however, correctly ignores these – the question hasn't asked about them.

If a source is biased in some way and reveals the writer's attitudes, don't assume that this is always a disadvantage. By showing us what the writer's opinions were, we learn something important about the past, e.g. that some people feared war, distrusted the government, etc.

7 Questions about the value of a piece of source material

Re-read the source above and think this time about its *advantages* or *value* as a type of source. The points you might make now would include some of the following:

  (a) Government reports usually tried to describe things accurately.
  (b) They quote the witness's own words.
  (c) The Commissioners interviewed the people who knew most about conditions in mines.
  (d) The information is often very precise.
  (e) We learn about people's feelings.

Notice how there are a lot of possible advantages, just as there were a lot of possible disadvantages. Some questions may even ask you to write about both. They might be phrased like this:

To what extent do you think government reports (as in Source C) would be useful to a historian studying Britain during the first half of the nineteenth century?

The key words here are *to what extent*. These invite you to write about both advantages and disadvantages. You might like to try answering this question. Look at the points that have been suggested for both advantages and disadvantages. Try to put them together as one answer using your own words.

Sometimes you may be asked to discuss the value of both primary and secondary sources. It is a common mistake to assume that secondary sources are bound to be less useful than primary sources. Some secondary sources do have very little value. But others are based on a close study of relevant primary sources and are extremely useful, so don't jump to conclusions. Think carefully about each source on its own merits.

8 Questions on a group of linked sources

Most of the evidence questions we have looked at so far have been based on only one piece of source material. GCSE exam papers are also likely to include questions on a group of linked sources. In some cases there may be as many as eight – usually of different kinds, e.g. photographs, cartoons, and different types of written sources.

Many of the questions are likely to ask you to compare one source with another. You might be asked to identify differences and similarities between accounts of a particular event. (Look again at the example on pages 20–21.) This might include identifying different attitudes or viewpoints. It might also require you to comment on whether particular sources are likely to be more or less reliable than others.

These questions are often more demanding than some of the ones you have read about earlier, because you will have to relate lots of

different considerations to each other. Practi̇~~~~
more confident about doing this. Have a look at
questions on page 66. See if you can answer *(a)* an~~~~
at the sources very carefully. Fix the main points of ̮~~~~
mind. Then re-read Source B and, as you do so, underlin̮~~~~
that agree with what is said in Source A.

Your list should read something like this:

great city;
wide streets;
the streets can be divided into the principal (or main) ones and the
  less important ones;
most streets are bordered by water.

Now write up your answer as two or three sentences. Having done this,
try the same thing with part *(b)*, which asks you to compare Source C
and Source A. If you tackle these questions step by step in a systematic
way, they will become much more manageable. You will find many
more questions of this type among the practice questions.

STIMULUS QUESTIONS

Some questions based on pieces of source material will be of a different
type altogether. These are often known as stimulus questions. In such
questions, the source material is used as a stimulus, i.e. something on
which to base questions, something to jog your memory. You are *not*
asked to use the source material as evidence, or to comment on its value,
reliability, etc. This example of a stimulus question is taken from a
MEG specimen paper:

This extract concerns the Munich Agreement of September, 1938.

We, the German Fuhrer and Chancellor, and the British Prime Minister,
have had a further meeting today and are agreed in recognising that
the question of Anglo-German relations is of the first importance for
the two countries and for Europe.

We regard the agreement signed last night and the Anglo-German Naval
Agreement as symbolic of the desire of our two peoples never to go to
war with one another again.

We are resolved that the method of consultation shall be the method
adopted to deal with other questions that may concern our two
countries, and we are determined to continue our efforts to remove
possible sources of difference and thus to contribute to assure the
peace of Europe.

...me the two men who signed this Agreement. *(2)*

(ii) Name two other statesmen who took part in the Munich Conference. *(2)*

(b) Describe the events of 1938, which led to the Munich Agreement. *(6)*

(c) Why did this Agreement fail to prevent the outbreak of war in 1939? *(15)*

$$\overline{25}$$

Even though you can tackle these questions without much reference to the stimulus, always read the sources very carefully. Their purpose is to help you, by reminding you of things you might otherwise have forgotten. In all other ways, however, the questions here are very similar to the short-answer questions and essay questions you studied in section 5.

PRACTICE QUESTIONS

Many of these questions don't require any background knowledge of the historical period to which they refer. Whatever syllabus you are following, you ought to be able to make something of them. Read through them all – to give you an idea of the kinds of questions you are going to have to answer in the exam. Try to answer at least some of them – either by jotting down notes or by writing out your answers in full.

1 Read Sources A and B and look at Source C.

(a) List *three* ways in which Source B agrees with Source A. *(3)*

(b) List *three* ways in which Source C agrees with Source A. *(3)*

(c) If you wished to check the accuracy of Source A, which would be more useful to you: Source B or Source C? Explain your choice. *(4)*

(d) Is it necessary to check the accuracy and reliability of Source A? Give reasons for your answer with reference to the Source. *(4)*

Source A

The great city of Tenochtitlan is built on a salt lake and from the mainland to the city is a distance of *2 leagues*. It has three approaches by means of *artificial causeways* .... The city is as large as *Seville* or *Cordoba*. Its streets (I speak of the *principal* ones) are very broad and straight; some of these and all the other roads are bordered by canals on which they go about in canoes. All the streets have gaps at regular intervals and at all these openings there are bridges ....

The city has many squares where markets are held and trading is carried on. There is one square twice as large as that of *Salamanca*. A very fine building in a great square serves as a kind of court .... The great city contains many temples or houses for idols, very beautiful buildings, situated in different districts ... (and) many large and fine buildings .... All have very delightful flower gardens of every kind.

(Hernan Cortes to Charles V, King of Spain, 30 October 1520)

2 leagues: about 6 miles
artificial causeways: man-made raised roads
Seville, Cordoba, Salamanca: cities in Spain
principal: main

Source B

The great city of Tenochtitlan has and had many wide and handsome streets; of these two or three are the principal ones and all others are formed half of earth like a brick pavement and the other half of water so that they can go along the land or by water in the boats and canoes.

(The Anonymous Conqueror's account)

Source C

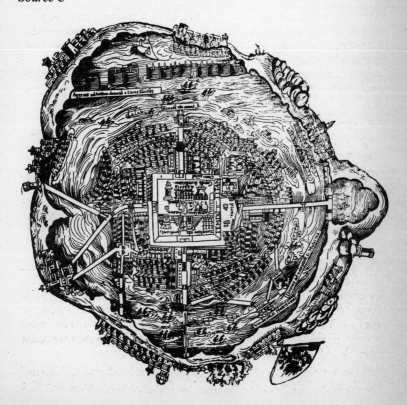

A drawing of Tenochtitlan, printed and published in Germany in 1524 and based on a sketch by Cortes.

(LEAG, June 1985, Joint 'O' level/CSE Schools Council History Project)

2 Study Sources G and H and then answer questions *(a)* and *(b)* which follow.

Source G

Philip Henry, a seventeen-year-old boy writing in his diary

(As the axe fell, there was) . . . such a groan as I never heard before, and desire I may never hear again.

Immediately the King was dead two troops of horses . . . advanced into the crowd which dispersed before them with remarkable speed saving themselves as well as they could from the horses' hooves by dodging up side lanes and alleys.

Source H

The Great Rebellion, V. Crinnion, Macmillan, 1984

The crowd surged forward . . . They were inhumanly barbarous to his dead corpse. His hair and blood were sold by parcels. Their hands and sticks were tinged by his blood and the block now cut into chips, as also the sand sprinkled with his sacred blood, were exposed for sale.

Philip Henry was an eye-witness and V. Crinnion is a modern writer.

(a) What differences are there between these two accounts of the events immediately following the execution?

(b) How do you account for this apparent disagreement?

(NEA, May 1985, Schools Council Project: 13–16)

3 Study Sources 11, 12 and 13 and then answer questions *(a)* to *(g)* below.

Study Source 11.

(a) Give *two* features of the electoral system in Britain before 1832 which are shown in this source. (2)

(b) From your own knowledge of the period, say whether this election was typical of the time. Explain your answer. (3)

(c) How useful would this source be to someone studying elections before the 1832 Reform Act? (2)

Study Source 12.

(d) What is the attitude of the cartoonist to Reform? Explain your answer. (2)

Study Source 13.

(e) In what way does this source contradict the impression of Reformers given in Source 12? (3)

(f) From the sources and your own knowledge explain this apparent contradiction. *(4)*

(g) What happened to the Procession when it reached St Peter's Fields? *(2)*

Source 11

I was unanimously elected by the elector to represent this ancient borough in Parliament . . . there was no other candidate, no opposition, no poll demanded . . . so I had nothing to do but thank the said elector . . . . On Friday morning I shall quit this triumphant scene with flying colours and a noble determination not to see it again in less than seven years.

(Francis Letters, Vol. II p. 493 relating to the election in Appleby of 1802)

Source 12

DEATH or LIBERTY! or Britannia & the Virtues of the Constitution in danger of Violation from the great Political Libertines Radical Reform

Source 13

From the windows of Mr Baxter's House . . . I saw the main body proceeding towards St Peter's Fields, and never saw a gayer spectacle. The 'marching order' of which so much was said afterwards, was what we so often see now in the processions of Sunday School children. . . . Our company laughed at the fears of the magistrates, and the remark was, that if the men intended mischief, they would not have brought their wives, their sisters, or their children with them.

(Description of procession to St Peter's Fields, Manchester, 16 August 1819 from 'Historical Sketches and Personal Recollections' by Prentice.)

(LEAG, June 1985, Schools Council History Project)

4 Look carefully at Sources A to E and answer the questions which follow.

THE NEW DEAL, 1933–9

Historians and others have long debated how far the New Deal, introduced by President Roosevelt, in his first term of office, can be judged a success. The following extracts illustrate some aspects of social and economic life in the USA during the 1930s.

Read the following extracts carefully and answer the questions.

Source A
This extract is taken from a novel, *The Grapes of Wrath*, which recounts the struggle of a farmer from Oklahoma who is trying to reach California after he has been ruined by the dust bowl.

He drove his car into a town. He scoured the farms for work. Where can we sleep the night?

Well there's Hooverville on the edge of the river. There's a whole raft of Okies there.

He drove his old car to Hooverville. He never asked again, for there was a Hooverville on the edge of every town.

The rag town lay close to the water; and the houses were tents, and weed-thatched enclosures, paper houses, a great junk pile. The man drove his family in and became a citizen of Hooverville – always they were called Hooverville. The man put up his own tent as near to the water as he could get; or if he had no tent, he went to the city dump and brought back cartons and built a house of corrugated paper.

Source B
A Saturday Evening Post reporter visits a working-class area of the city of Boston in order to see why Roosevelt had polled so many votes there in the 1940 election.

William J. Galvin, the Democratic ward leader, has a simple explanation for the Roosevelt vote: 'Probably no section in the country gained more under the New Deal'. Out of the population of 30 000, hundreds got pay rises under the wage–hour law; hundreds of seasonal workers are having slack months cushioned by unemployment insurance benefits. The NYA is helping 300–500 youths: at the worst of the depression thousands held WPA jobs; 600 old people receive old-age assistance; another 600 are on direct relief and get aid for dependent children. Charlestown is a depressed area; the WPA improved its bathing beach; a new low-cost housing project will relieve some of the area's over-crowding.

Nearly one half of those of voting age are under forty. Their economic memories begin with Hoover. Galvin's two younger brothers left school and went into CCC camps during the depression. They are now working as labourers in the nearby Boston Navy Yard, which has quadrupled its employment in recent months.

Source C
Barton J. Bernstein, in his book *Towards a New Past*, argues that the New Deal was less successful, in some ways, than many Americans had accepted. His book was published in 1969.

The New Deal neglected many Americans – sharecroppers, tenant farmers, farm labourers and migratory workers, unskilled workers and the unemployed Negroes. They were left outside the new order.

Sources D and E
The next two Extracts are graphs illustrating the levels of unemployment and of national income in the period from the beginning of 1929 to the end of 1941.

Source D

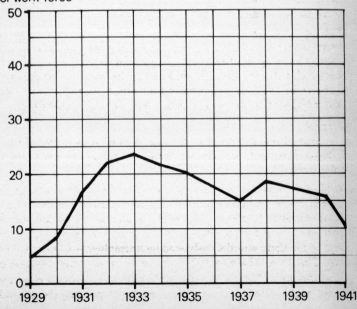

Unemployment 1929-41

National Income 1929-41

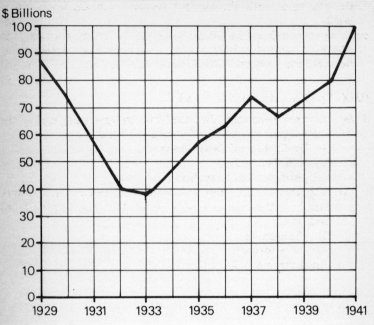

$ Billions

QUESTIONS

1 *(a)* In Source B, what is meant by the initials WPA and CCC? *(2)*

  (b) In Source A, why are the shanty towns 'always called Hoover-villes'? *(3)*

2 *(a)* At the end of which year did unemployment in the USA reach its highest level? (Refer to Source D.) *(1)*

  (b) Was this before or after the beginning of Roosevelt's first term of office? *(1)*

3 *(a)* Examine Source E. In which year was there the greatest increase in National Income? *(1)*

  (b) What information is given in Source B, which helps explain such an increase in National Income? *(2)*

4 *(a)* To which two groups listed in Source C might the man in Source A have belonged? *(2)*

  (b) Why did the first four groups listed in Source C *not* benefit from the Agricultural Adjustment Acts? *(4)*

5 The newspaper report (Source B) is a much more valuable source to the historian as evidence of social life in the USA during the 1930s than is Source A, taken from a novel.

Do you agree with the above statement? Explain your answer briefly. *(8)*

6 Using information from all the sources, give arguments to explain why Roosevelt's New Deal was not completely successful in solving the social and economic difficulties facing the USA in the 1930s. *(6)*

Total marks 30

(MEG, Specimen examination paper)

5 *(a)* What problems might face the historian when using *each* of the following primary sources for the First World War:
   (i)   letters from soldiers at the front;
   (ii) official bulletins;
   (iii) poems written by soldiers.

 (b) Comment on the value to the historian of twentieth-century British political history of *each* of the following types of evidence:
   (i)   photographs;
   (ii) oral evidence;
   (iii) the memoirs of politicians.

SECTION 7

How to tackle the coursework

MARKS AND REGULATIONS

In every GCSE History syllabus, at least 20% of the final assessment will consist of the marks you have received for various pieces of coursework. (The only people to whom this won't apply are the small number of *external candidates*, mentioned in section 1.) Most candidates will therefore be putting a lot of effort into the different pieces of coursework that are going to be taken into account. This section will try to help you do your best in this important part of the assessment.

The proportion of the total marks given for coursework will vary from one GCSE syllabus to another. The lower limit of 20% is laid down in the History Criteria, but there is no upper limit. In theory, it could account for 100% of the marks. In practice, however, many syllabuses will give either 30% or 40% of the marks to coursework, and 30% will be more common than 40%. Whatever the proportion of marks, your performance in this part of the assessment may make a very big difference to your final grade.

All GCSE History syllabuses provide detailed regulations about coursework. These will tell your teachers when the coursework marks have to be sent off to the exam group, what sorts of objectives coursework assignments are supposed to test, how they are to be marked, and so on. Sometimes these regulations will be published along with all the syllabus details. Sometimes they will be issued in a separate booklet. In some cases it may be possible to buy copies of these regulations from the exam group (see page 6). Most people will receive all the information they need from their teachers. Listen very carefully when instructions about these coursework assignments are being given. Take a note of everything that you will need to know. If you're not sure about what you have to do, keep on asking your teacher until you are quite clear. Often you will be given a printed handout with all the detailed instructions you need.

Questions about coursework

These are the questions about coursework that everyone should be able to answer:

1 How many pieces of coursework will count for this part of the assessment?
The number will vary considerably from one syllabus to another.

2 What are the word limits for each piece of coursework?
These will always be fairly approximate, e.g. 'between 1200 and 2000 words' or 'around 1000 words'. It won't usually matter if you are slightly under or over the limit. You should begin to worry, however, if you are writing a lot more or a lot less than you are asked to do. In the first case, you are likely to be penalised for not writing concisely enough. In the second, you are unlikely to be able to deal with the topic in sufficient depth unless you write a bit more. Find out whether the word limits include footnotes, bibliographies (lists of books and materials consulted) and sources that you have quoted. This can make an enormous difference.

3 Can all coursework assignments be done in your own time or do some of them have to be completed in class?
Some syllabuses may require that one or more of the coursework assignments is done in class, but others may not insist on this. To some extent this will be up to your teacher and your school to decide.

4 When will coursework assignments have to be handed in?
If you are doing quite a lot of the work at home on your own, it is particularly important to know what your deadlines are going to be. Knowing this well in advance will help you plan your work so that you don't have to rush to get it finished at the last minute. This is especially important if you are doing coursework assignments for other subjects as well.

5 What are the regulations about the way coursework is to be presented?
These will vary from one examining group to another. It is important to know what they are and to do things in the way in which you are asked to do them. The regulations used by the NEA in one of its syllabuses can be found on pages 77-8.

6 Can some of the coursework assignments take the form of work that is not written?
Is there any restriction on the number of these assignments? Can they take any form, e.g. tape-recordings, photographs, models, computer programmes, films, diagrams, dramatic reconstructions? Does non-written work like this have to be accompanied by some written statement explaining what it is all about, and why and how it was done?

7 What are the objectives that each coursework assignment is trying to encourage?

Some assignments might be concerned mainly with getting you to use your skills in handling evidence. Others might be more concerned with your ability to see things from the perspective of people in the past. Some might be a combination of the two – though with one or other of the objectives being the main one. If you know what the purpose of an assignment is, you will have a much better idea about how to tackle it.

8 How will these coursework assignments be marked?

What proportion of marks will go to the various objectives? Will a certain proportion of marks be given for English and presentation? Again, it is very useful to know these things.

COURSEWORK EXAMPLES

On the next few pages, we set out two examples of what GCSE History coursework is likely to involve.

Example 1

The first example is from the NEA's Modern World syllabus, as used in the 1987 Joint 'O' level/CSE examination.

INTERNAL ASSESSMENT OF COURSEWORK

Allocation of marks 30%

Coursework will be assessed by the candidate's teacher, and will be *statistically moderated* (brought into line with the examination in various ways) by the boards of NEA.

Coursework assignments will be based on Themes 4 and 5, 'Colonialism' and 'Human Rights' respectively. For Theme 4, a candidate's work should be based on a study of any *one* area of the world to illustrate all the given aspects of colonialism. For Theme 5 *one* of the five subsections should be studied.

Each candidate will be required to submit a minimum of *four* and a maximum of *six* assignments, a minimum of *two* of which should be based on each of Themes 4 and 5.

Theme 4: Colonialism
A candidate's work should be based on a study of any *one* area of the world to illustrate *all* the following aspects of colonialism:

　　(a) **The pre-colonial experience**
　　(b) **The origins of colonialism**
　　(c) **The colonial experience**
　　(d) **The growth of nationalism**

(e) The achievement of independence

(f) Post-independence

Theme 5: Human rights

A candidate's work should be based on *one* of the following:

(a) Religious divisions in Ireland from the mid-nineteenth century to the present day

(b) The Jews 1880 to the present day

(c) The changing position of women in Britain

(d) Civil Rights in the USA

(e) Apartheid in South Africa

THE ASSESSMENT OF COURSEWORK

(a) *Requirements*

To fulfil the coursework requirements, candidates must submit a minimum of *four* and a maximum of *six* assignments which *must be related to the syllabus*. If candidates are to be considered for the award of the higher marks, they will normally be expected to satisfy a total minimum requirement of 3000 written words. Consequently more than 6000 words will not normally be expected.

Assignments must be available for monitoring purposes by 31st March in the year of the examination.

(b) *Assessment Objectives*

The assignments will be marked by the candidate's teacher according to the following assessment criteria:

The candidate's ability to

1 collect and collate information in relation to a particular historical problem or topic;

2 interpret and evaluate a variety of historical sources, both primary and secondary, by distinguishing between fact, opinion and judgement and by detecting deficiences such as gaps, inconsistencies and bias;

3 reconstruct past events as seen from the perspective of people in the past;

4 make use of historical information in order to demonstrate an understanding of the concepts of cause and consequence, continuity and change, similarity and difference.

(c) *Presentation*

The Boards are anxious that both candidates and their teachers should enjoy freedom of choice in methods and styles of presentation. Teachers are reminded however that it will be necessary to include work in a variety of formats to show the range of historical skills required to fulfil the above assessment criteria. The following are suggestions as to the sort of work which might be included:

work on the role of individuals in the past,
work arising from visits,
diaries,
work on all kinds of source material,
local history.

imaginative reconstructions,
interpretation of maps, diagrams and statistics,
personal interviews.

Although it is expected that work will normally be presented in written form, the use of films, diagrams, models, tape-recordings and photographs – with adequate explanatory written material – is also to be encouraged. However, where non-written coursework is undertaken, some product must be retained by the centre for any subsequent monitoring requirements.

Test essays and class notes must *not* form a part of the coursework submitted for assessment.

Each candidate's assignments should normally be presented in a manilla file cover, clearly labelled with the candidate's name, centre name and centre number. Labels will be provided by the boards. *Ring binders should not be used.*

All coursework must be the candidate's own work. In particular, candidates must understand that to present material copied directly from books or other sources without acknowledgement, will be regarded as deliberate deception. Quotations should be properly marked and their source clearly indicated. A candidate must not be allowed to alter a piece of coursework in any way after the teacher has marked it and indicated errors or omissions.

For centres inside the NEA any candidate who uses or is suspected of using or attempting to use any unfair means is to be reported immediately to the Secretary of the home CSE Board. For centres outside the NEA the report must be made to the Secretary of the Joint Matriculation Board. If the boards are satisfied that an offence has been committed the candidate will be liable to disqualification.

Candidates should be made aware of this and each candidate will be required to complete and sign a declaration form to certify that all the coursework submitted for assessment is the candidate's own. Forms will be supplied by the boards.

(d) Marking
The four assessment criteria carry an equal weighting of 15 marks each and consequently the coursework assignments are to be marked out of a total of 60. At least 5 and not more than 15 marks

must be reserved for an objective when tested in an individual assignment. No more than *two* objectives should be tested in any one assignment. An individual assignment should carry at least 10 but not more than 20 of the total marks available. Examples of coursework assignments and mark weightings are provided on the specimen Coursework Proposal Sheets.

NORTHERN EXAMINING ASSOCIATION Joint GCE 'O'-level and CSE examinations
Coursework proposal sheet

| | | **HISTORY (Modern World)** |

This form is to be completed and sent to ALSEB, 12, Harter Street, Manchester, M1 6HL by 15 February of the FIRST year of the course.

Centre Name and Address	Centre Number
	Year of Exam
Post Code	

The centre must retain a copy of this proposal for reference purposes.

If there is more than one assessment set for the centre state whether this is sheet 1 of 2, 2 of 2 etc. ..... of .....

Assessment set (A, B, C etc.) ....

Indicate in the table how marks will be awarded. At least 5, and not more than 15 marks must be reserved for each of the four criteria.

Approximate no. of Candidates in Assessment set ....

	Details of how marks will be awarded				
Title of each assignment *(Full details of all assignments must be provided overleaf)*	Criterion 1 Min. 5 marks Max. 15 marks	Criterion 2 Min. 5 marks Max. 15 marks	Criterion 3 Min. 5 marks Max. 15 marks	Criterion 4 Min. 5 marks Max. 15 marks	Actual assignment mark (between 10 & 20)
1 GANDHI	10				10
2 NEHRU AND MODERNISATION			10		10
3 THE EASTER RISING 1916		10			10
4 LIFE ON THE FALLS ROAD			5	5	10
5 * THE ASSASSINATION OF MRS GANDHI		5		5	10
6 * THE CIVIL RIGHTS MOVEMENT 1964 -72	5			5	10
TOTALS	15	15	15	15	60
* Optional					

Not more than 2 criteria are to be assessed in any ONE assignment.

DETAILS OF ASSIGNMENTS

Theme 4: Colonialism

1 Gandhi

Using a variety of references (mostly from School Library) and a collection of source material, candidates are required to produce: (a) a biographical sketch, and (b) an assessment of the importance of Gandhi in achieving independence in India.

2 Nehru and modernisation

Candidates produce two statements on Nehru's policies in the period up to 1964. One defends, the other attacks, the policy of Nehru's Government.

3 **The Easter Rising, 1916**

Based on a collection of sources on the Easter Rising in 1916. Ten questions aim to elicit comprehension, analysis and evaluation of the sources.

4 **Life on the Falls Road**

An inhabitant of Belfast explains how the city has changed over the 20 years to 1980. Candidates can choose a sectarian or political allegiance. The assignment is written after a class debate in which prepared positions are argued.

5 **The assassination of Mrs Gandhi**

Ten questions are based on a collection of sources on Indira Gandhi's assassination. Five of the questions require analysis, particularly with regard to bias. The other five invite comparisons with earlier examples of trouble between Hindus and Sikhs in India.

6 **The Civil Rights Movement 1964–72**

Candidates are provided with a number of sources and pieces of information relating to the Civil Rights Movement. These are ordered in such a way as to provide a framework for an essay showing how the Unionists and Loyalists responded to the movement. Candidates do their own reference work to explain the context of the sources of information.

Notice how each assignment is carefully related to the various assessment objectives (or criteria). For example, the assignment on the assassination of Mrs Gandhi is designed to test both objective *2* and objective *4*. Look at these two objectives again. They both have the same weighting, i.e. 5 marks for objective *2* and 5 marks for objective *4*. Knowing this should help you to avoid spending too much time on one part of the assignment at the expense of the other.

Notice also that each of these assignments 'must be the candidate's own work' and that you will be required to sign a declaration to this effect. All GCSE syllabuses are likely to include the same regulation. This doesn't mean, in most cases, that you can't discuss the assignment with your teacher, with your parents or with your friends. It does mean, however, that when you come to write up your assignment it will be *you* who is doing it – and in your own words. It is sometimes useful to quote other people's views, but if you do so, always indicate that these are not your words, i.e. acknowledge the quote and say where it was taken from. This is what good historians always do. It also makes clear that you aren't pretending that you wrote something that was actually written by someone else. You can either show that you are quoting by indenting the quoted words, i.e. starting the lines further in from the edge of the page, or by using inverted commas. Whichever you do, you should also give further information about the source of your quotation in a footnote. An example of such a footnote might be: **1** Glyndwr Williams, *The Expansion of Europe in the Eighteenth Century* (London, 1966) p.284. You can see that five pieces of information are needed: the author's name, the title of the work, the place of publication, the date of publication, and the page reference.

At the end of the assignment you should normally also provide a brief bibliography. This is simply a list of the books you have used in preparing that assignment. It will obviously include any books you have quoted in the course of your answer, and also any other books that you have used. This might be the bibliography at the end of an assignment, based on source material, about the rise of Hitler in Germany:

Bibliography
Richard Grunberger, *Germany 1918–1945* (London, 1964) ch. 5.
John Martell, *The Twentieth Century World* (London, 1980) ch. 6.
William L. Shirer, *Berlin Diary* (London, 1941) pp.30–5.
Albert Speer, *Inside the Third Reich* (London, 1971) Part One.

Make a note of all this information as you go along. It can be a nuisance having to chase after books that you have already returned to the library or lent to a friend.

Example 2

The second example of what GCSE History coursework is likely to involve is from the LEAG Joint 'O' level/CSE syllabus based on the Schools History Project.

Coursework accounts for 40% of the total assessment of this Syllabus and includes work from all sections of the Syllabus except the Study in Development. The Modern World Study and History Around Us are assessed by coursework only. It is therefore essential that coursework objectives are met and that the nature of the work is clear so that it can be *moderated*. Not all the work set in any one section will be designed specifically to meet coursework objectives: there may well be background information, notes, tests and other exercises which are a necessary part of the course but which should not be counted in the overall marks and need not be submitted for moderation. What is finally assessed and submitted for moderation should clearly meet coursework objectives and provide a representative sample of the student's work. Work on which students are assessed will therefore be work which is central to the Course.

Moderated: **one school's coursework being compared with the course-**

work from other schools, to make sure that, among other things, they are all being marked at the same standard.

A COURSEWORK INSTRUCTIONS

1 The units should be divided as follows:

Unit	Assignments	Total length	*%Assessment
Modern World Studies	Either 1 or 2	Approx. 1250 to 2000 words	10%
Enquiry in Depth	Either 1 or 2	Approx. 1250 to 2000 words	10%
History Around Us	Either 2 or 3	Approx. 2500 to 3000 words	20%
Total	4–7	Approx. 5000 to 7000 words	40%

*Throughout this document the mark allocation is expressed as a percentage of the whole assessment.

2 Coursework Objectives
All the objectives listed below should be covered in the total coursework of each candidate. Any single assignment may relate to one or more objectives.

(a) Analysis of causation and motivation.
(b) Interpretation of current situation in the context of past events.
(c) Empathetic reconstruction of the ways of thinking, ideas, attitudes and beliefs characteristics of a different time and place.
(d) Analysis of the role of the individual in history.
(e) Personal investigation and description of a site.
(f) Relation of a site to its historical context.
(g) An understanding of the historical evidence available and an assessment of the value of such evidence.

3 At least 2½% and no more than 7½% should be reserved for each objective.

4 A maximum of 22½% is available to be allocated to other objectives selected by the teacher, provided these are consistent with the Syllabus philosophy. Such other objectives must be listed by the teacher on the Coursework Assessment Form. Possible examples include:

relation of Modern World Studies topic to wide global context;
correlation of visual and documentary evidence;
ability to follow and comment on a current news item.

The weighting of each teacher-selected objective should also be in the range 2½–7½%.

Teachers wishing to add their own objectives are strongly advised to write to the Board with whom they intend to make their examination entry.

COURSEWORK ASSESSMENT FORM

Centre Name: Riverside Comprehensive   Centre No. 34481

Candidate No.: ....   Candidate Name and initials Mark Allsation (Mrs Morgan)

OBJECTIVES (160 marks)		Coursework objectives (see below)							Teacher-selected objectives			TOTAL	
		(a)	(b)	(c)	(d)	(e)	(f)	(g)	(h)	(i)	(k)	T'chr	Mod.
Assignment	Maxima	20	10	30	20	30	30	10	10			160	
MODERN WORLD STUDIES (40 marks)	A	10		10								20	
	B		10						10			20	
ENQUIRY IN DEPTH (40 marks)	C	10		10								20	
	D				10		10					20	
HISTORY AROUND US (80 marks)	E					30						30	
	F			10	10							20	
	G						30					30	
TOTALS (Teacher)		20	10	30	20	30	30	10	10			160	
TOTALS (Moderator)													

Objectives (a) - (g). These are listed in the Coursework Instructions.

Teacher-selected objectives:

(h) Ability to follow and comment upon a current news item for 2 or 3 weeks.

(i) ....

(k) ....

Notice again how assignments are closely related to particular objectives. Objective *(a)*, for example, relates to analysis of causation and motivation, i.e. why things happen and why people in the past acted in particular ways. If your Modern World assignment A is just concerned with saying how things happened - rather than why they happened - you won't be satisfying the objective. You are unlikely, therefore, to receive many of the 10 marks allocated to that objective in that particular assignment. Objective *(b)* asks for *interpretation*. If your Modern World assignment B consists of just a collection of newspaper cuttings about some recent event and makes no attempt to explain or interpret this event, then again it will receive few marks – however thick the file and however beautifully presented. Objective *(c)* asks you to enter into the ways of thinking of *a different time and place*. If you just concentrate on the ways in which people in a past period were like people today, you will have missed out a vital part of the exercise. Again you are unlikely to receive high marks. Objective *(d)* asks for an *analysis* of the individual's role. Biographies (accounts of the life of an individual) that don't relate this life to other developments, will not satisfy the objective. All this emphasises the importance of knowing what the purpose of each assignment is and making sure that everything you write helps to achieve that purpose in one way or another. Keep on asking yourself: What is the question trying to get me to do? Am I doing it?

You will notice in both the NEA and the LEAG coursework examples that marks were not specifically given for presentation. Poor presentation, however, is bound to detract from the impression that your work gives. Pay particular attention to spelling. With most coursework there is little excuse for persistent mis-spelling of words. You should have a dictionary and keep on using it to check the spelling of any words you are not too sure about. Be particularly careful about specifically historical words, e.g. 'Lenin' has one middle 'n', not two; 'Khrushchev' has three 'h's; 'appeasement' has an 'e' in the middle. Remember all the rules of punctuation: full stops and capital letters for sentences; inverted commas for quotations (whether from books or of speech); the use of commas to break up long sentences; the division of longer answers into paragraphs. Write neatly and legibly. Make sure that all maps and diagrams are carefully drawn and labelled. (With maps, don't forget about the scale.) Label all pictures and photographs (and give a footnote reference to show which book or magazine each one came from). Think about layout – especially with longer assignments. Work out the best places in the text to put the illustrations, use sub-headings, and provide a list of contents. As with so much else, it's largely a question of careful attention to detail. This, in fact, is one of the historian's most important skills. If you show care in your presentation, you're likely to be demonstrating it in other ways as well.

SECTION 8
How your work is marked

Once the exam is over, you'll probably just want to forget about it until the results are announced. You'll want to do all the things you haven't been able to do while you have been revising. You'll try *not* to think what is happening to your examination script in the meantime. You might be just a little bit curious, however, about how your script is going to be marked. This section will try to tell you – very briefly – what this involves.

MARKING SCHEMES

Each examining group employs a team of examiners (or markers) whose job is to mark all your scripts. These examiners are all experienced history teachers – though not of course people who know anything about you. They are given a marking scheme to guide them and to make sure that they all mark in the same way and according to the same standard. It should not make any difference which examiner marks your script. The marking scheme will tell the examiners how many marks are to be awarded to each question and to each part of each question. You may even know what these are yourself – they're sometimes given on the exam paper.

Examiners will also be told what kinds of answers they should expect, e.g. for full marks, for half marks, and so on. What they will be looking for are signs that the assessment objectives for the various sections have been satisfied, e.g. that in source-based questions you can identify bias and point to inconsistencies, and that in essay questions you are able to construct a good argument. You will rarely be marked just on how many accurate facts you happen to know.

Here are two examples of marking schemes for GCSE questions to give you a general idea of how the marking is likely to be done. Level One, as you can see, is the lowest level; Level Four is the highest.

Imagine you are a Red Guard in Petrograd in 1917. Write an account of your part in the events of October–November 1917. In the course of

your answer, explain why you joined the Red Guards and describe your hopes for the new Russia that you are helping to create.   *(20 marks)*

MARKING SCHEME

Level One: Gives a factual account (with some inaccuracies) of the October–November Revolution in Petrograd, indicating that, in a general way, people in that period had distinctive feelings, attitudes etc., without being very precise about what these were.

OR

Makes passing reference to one or two attitudes that might have been held by a member of the Red Guards, but shows very limited knowledge and understanding of the events of October–November 1917 in Petrograd.   *(0–4 marks)*

Level Two: Gives a substantially accurate account of the October–November Revolution, indicating some understanding (though limited) of both motives [why he or she joined] and *hopes*.   *(5–9 marks)*

Level Three: Accurate account of October–November 1917 Revolution focusing on the specific part played by the Red Guards, linked with a reasonably full statement of motives and *hopes*.   *(10–14 marks)*

Level Four: Accurate account of October–November, focused on Red Guards, together with an examination of motives and *hopes* that indicates that these might be varied and complex. The whole answer also shows an attempt by the candidate to go back in imagination to a world with values and attitudes in many ways very different from those of most people in late twentieth-century Britain.   *(15–20 marks)*

Notice that you are being marked on your ability to satisfy the assessment objective for this kind of question: 'to show an ability to look at events and issues from the perspective of people in the past'.

The second example is of the marking scheme for one of the subquestions based on the cartoon shown here. The Budget referred to in the cartoon was introduced by Lloyd George (Chancellor of the Exchequer) in 1909. The cartoon was issued by the Conservative Party.

Referring in detail to the cartoon, describe the cartoonist's attitude towards the Budget.   *(10 marks)*

MARKING SCHEME

Level One: Understands that the cartoonist is hostile to the Budget, without necessarily appreciating the reason for this hostility or the detailed ways in which this hostility is expressed in the cartoon.*(1 mark)*

Level Two: Understands that the cartoonist's hostility to the Budget is related to budget proposals for increased taxation.   *(2–3 marks)*

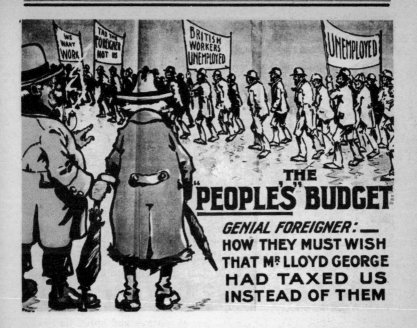

THE "PEOPLE'S" BUDGET

GENIAL FOREIGNER: —
HOW THEY MUST WISH
THAT Mr LLOYD GEORGE
HAD TAXED US
INSTEAD OF THEM

Level Three: Understands that the cartoonist's hostility to the Budget is related to increased taxation and that this increased taxation is assumed to harm the British workers via its damaging effect on employment.

(4–5 marks)

Level Four: Understands that the cartoonist, via his attacks on the harm likely to be done by the Budget, is also advocating tariff reform (i.e. 'Tax the foreigner', the introduction of taxes on imported goods).

(6–7 marks)

Level Five: Understands that the cartoon is propaganda both against the Budget and in favour of tariff reform and comments on the link between this position and the known attitudes of the Conservative Party at this time. *(8–10 marks)*

Notice here that higher marks are awarded for answers that *(a)* describe *precisely* what the cartoonist's attitude is and *(b)* think about the *implications* of what is happening (e.g. the support for tariff reform), i.e. don't just state the obvious.

To do well here, you will need to *look* very closely, *think* about what you see, *think again* about what you see, and then *organise* your thoughts.

You will have noticed that these marking schemes allow the examiner a certain amount of freedom within each of the levels. If you reach

Level Five in the second example, you will get 8, 9 or 10 marks, depending on how well you have satisfied the requirements for that particular level. An answer might get 8 marks, for example, if it fails to back up comments on the cartoonist's support for tariff reform with detailed references to the cartoon itself. Examiners also have to use their own judgement when they come across an answer that is obviously very good but which doesn't do things in quite the way that the marking scheme asks for. Answers like this should still get the high marks they deserve.

In practice, marking schemes are often altered in the early stages of marking – in order to take into account what you (the candidates) have actually written. This is one of the main reasons why all the examiners get together in a meeting to discuss how the exam paper is going to be marked. At the end of this meeting they should go away with a clear idea of what each question is asking for and how many marks different kinds of answers should receive. To make sure that they continue to mark in the same way, the marking is always closely supervised by Chief Examiners. Their job is to make sure that everyone is marking to the same standard. If for some reason this isn't happening, scripts will be adjusted or re-marked. No system is perfect, but you can be confident that every effort is made to ensure that your answers are marked carefully and fairly.

YOUR EXAM GRADE

The total marks that you will receive for GCSE History will be worked out from your coursework marks and from the marks that you got on the various exam papers. Your coursework will have been marked in a similar way to the exam papers, i.e. with a carefully drawn up marking scheme. A check will also have been kept to make sure that different schools are marking at the same standard. Where this isn't happening, adjustments will be made, e.g. the marks will be scaled up or down as necessary. The total marks (i.e. for exam and coursework) will then be converted into a grade on the scale A–G (see section 1).

Every effort will be made to ensure that candidates are awarded a grade C in one year for work that is the same as that needed for a grade C in the previous year. In deciding how many marks you need to obtain a particular grade, Chief Examiners may well take into account whether examination papers were slightly more difficult or slightly easier than in previous years. They might look at scripts from previous years just to make absolutely sure that the various grades are being awarded for the same level of work. Once the marks are turned into grades, Chief Examiners may also look at scripts very close to the borderline between grades – just to check again that people are getting the grades they deserve. If grade C goes from 60 to 69 (this is just an imaginary example), scripts with a mark of 69, for example, may well be looked at again to see if they deserve a B instead.

Mistakes are very rare indeed – considering the vast number of papers that are marked each year. If, after careful thought, your school thinks that a mistake might have been made in *your* case, it has the right to appeal against the grade you have received. What happens in this situation is that the script is re-marked by one of the Chief Examiners. Usually he or she finds that the marking, addition etc. are perfectly correct. Very occasionally a mistake has been made. In this small number of cases, the exam board admits its mistake and changes the grades.

Grade descriptions

As yet, it is not laid down precisely what abilities you will need to show in order to get a particular grade. The History Criteria give examples, though, of what might be expected of candidates at Grade F and at Grade C. These grade descriptions, as they are called, or some version of them, will be used for all GCSE History syllabuses. It is not expected that you will be able to meet all the demands equally well, and weaknesses in one area may well be offset by an above average performance in another. However, the descriptions give you a general idea of what you have to do in order to get these grades.

Grade descriptions are provided to give a general indication of the standards of achievement likely to have been shown by candidates awarded particular grades. The grade awarded will depend in practice upon the extent to which the candidate has met the assessment objectives over-all and it might conceal weakness in one aspect of the examination which is balanced by above average performance in some other.

6.1 Grade F
Candidates will be expected:

> *6.1.1* **to recall and display a limited amount of accurate and relevant historical knowledge; to show a basic understanding of the historical concepts of cause and consequence, continuity and change, sufficiently supported by obvious examples; to identify and list differences and similarities;**
>
> *6.1.2* **to display knowledge of perspectives of other people based on specific examples of situations and events;**
>
> *6.1.3* **to show ability to comprehend straightforward evidence; to extract partial and/or generalised information;**
>
> *6.1.4* **to demonstrate the obvious limitations of a particular piece of evidence needed to reconstruct a given historical event;**

6.1.5 to make simple comparisons between pieces of evidence; to list the major features of two or more pieces of evidence without drawing conclusions from it;

6.1.6 to communicate in an understandable form; to use simple historical terminology.

6.2 *Grade C*

Candidates will be expected:

6.2.1 to recall and use historical knowledge accurately and relevantly in support of a logical and evaluative argument; to distinguish between cause and occasion of an event; to show that change in History is not necessarily linear or 'progressive'; to compare and contrast people, events, issues and institutions; to demonstrate understanding of such concepts by deploying accurate though limited evidence;

6.2.2 to show an ability to look at events and issues from the perspective of other people in the past; to understand the importance of looking for motives;

6.2.3 to demonstrate comprehension of a range of evidence either by translating from one form to another (e.g. explaining accurately the information contained in a bar graph) or by summarising information given in a document; to answer accurately and fully questions demanding specific information to be extracted from the evidence;

6.2.4 to demonstrate the limitations of a particular piece of evidence; e.g. point to the use of emotive language and to generalisations based on little or no evidence; to indicate the other types of evidence that the historian would need to consult in relation to the topic and period in question;

6.2.5 to compare and contrast two or more different types of evidence and write a coherent conclusion based on them, though all aspects may not be taken into account;

6.2.6 to communicate clearly in a substantially accurate manner, making correct and appropriate use of historical terminology.

Some examining groups are developing descriptions of what you are expected to do for some of the other grades. This statement of what is expected of Grade A candidates is being used by the SEG for one of their History syllabuses.

Grade A
Candidates will be expected:

1 to recall and use historical knowledge accurately and relevantly in support of a logical and evaluative argument; to distinguish between cause and occasion of an event; to analyse and to synthesise historical problems with clarity and fluency; to show that change in history is not necessarily linear or 'progressive'; to compare and contrast people, events, issues and institutions;

2 to demonstrate understanding of historical concepts, to appreciate that many of them are complex, and to deploy accurate and relevant evidence;

3 to show an ability to look at events and issues from the perspective of other people in the past; to understand the importance of looking for motives; to display imagination in seeing the past through the eyes of those living at the time;

4 to demonstrate comprehension of a range of evidence either by translating from one form to another (e.g. explaining accurately the information contained in a bar graph) or by summarising information given in a document; to answer accurately and fully questions demanding specific information to be extracted from the evidence;

5 to demonstrate the limitations of a particular piece of evidence, e.g. point to the use of emotive language and to generalisations based on little or no evidence; to identify deficiencies in sources to indicate other types of evidence that the historian would need to consult in relation to the topic and period in question;

6 to compare and contrast two or more different types of evidence, showing where they contradict or support each other, and write a coherent conclusion based on them;

7 to communicate clearly and coherently in an accurate manner.

The Three Domains

There are plans to spell out even more precisely than this exactly what you will have to do in order to obtain a particular grade. History, for example, is likely to be divided up into three aspects (known as *domains*). These may well involve something like the following:

I Historical knowledge and understanding

This domain is concerned with candidates' ability to recall and select historical knowledge and to use historical skills and concepts to structure and communicate historical knowledge in ways that convey understanding of aspects of the past:

    (a) communicating narrative and description;
    (b) using concepts;
    (c) showing an ability to look at events and issues from the perspective of people in the past.

II Historical enquiry

This domain is concerned with the skills and techniques candidates will need to employ in gathering and recording historical evidence:

(a) preparing questions to acquire information;
(b) locating evidence;
(c) relating different types of evidence and recording findings.

III Historical reasoning

This domain is concerned with the skills and techniques candidates will need to employ in using a full range of historical evidence for a required purpose:

(a) assessing the utility of evidence;
(b) interpreting evidence;
(c) considering the reliability of evidence;
(d) reaching a judgement.

For each part of each of these domains, four levels will be identified (Level One being the lowest). These are the levels for 'Locating evidence' in Domain II:

Level Four: able to locate all readily available sources and derive information suitable to satisfy the demands of the task.
Level Three: able to locate a range of sources and derive information suitable to satisfy the demands of the task.
Level Two: able to locate an appropriate source and derive specific information from it.
Level One: able to locate an appropriate source and derive specific information from it, given guidance.

To get a Grade F, you might have to reach Level One (overall) in each of the three domains. To get a Grade C, you might have to reach Level Two in one of domains I or III and Level Three (or Four) in the other of domains I or III. The level you have reached in the different domains is also likely to be reported on your GCSE certificate. The details of these *grade criteria*, as they are called, have still to be worked out. Once they are introduced, they are bound to have an effect on how you are taught and how you are tested both in the exam and in coursework. Above all they will make it even clearer than it is already what are the objectives behind different types of questions, and what you will have to do in order to achieve these objectives. This is bound to help you in preparing for the examination.

EXAMINERS' REPORTS

From time to time examining groups publish reports on how candidates have done in particular examinations. These are usually written by the Chief Examiners, because they are the people who have read the largest number of scripts. They know better than anyone else which questions caused most problems, which historical inaccuracies were most common, and what candidates needed to do in order to obtain higher marks in their answers. These reports will usually be sent to all schools entering candidates for that group's examinations. If you can get hold of these, you will find that you are able to learn a great deal from other people's mistakes.

SECTION 9

A few last words

Answers. Remember there are three,
one each from section A and B
and one from those or section C,
though that one could be hard I reckon.
June Revision;
and the long days beckon.

This is the first verse of a poem called 'June Revision', by a young Scottish poet who is also a historian. It's about a history teacher giving last minute advice to his class before their exam. Much of the advice reads like the earlier chapters of this book. The class, however, is less than attentive. It's June and 'the long days beckon'. The students prefer to 'chatter'; their thoughts 'stray to love . . . and things that really matter'. You may well be feeling the same. The last weeks of revision can be very tiring. They can also be rather boring. Don't give up, though. Revision doesn't last for ever. You'll have the whole summer ahead of you, plenty of time for all the things you've had to neglect while you've been revising. If you have done everything this book has recommended, it will be a well-earned rest!

Forget about history for a while. But don't forget about it altogether. If your GCSE History course has done what it's supposed to do, you won't *want* to forget about it. It will have taught you that the past didn't just exist for the sake of getting through exams. It was full of real people like you and your friends. It was full of exciting events: things that have made you ashamed to be a human being, things that have made you proud to be a human being, ordinary things, and things stranger than anything you could ever have imagined. The past still shapes the way we behave today. It is all around us – in buildings and objects and landscapes. It's also inside our heads. In a sense we *are* the past, influenced in everything we do by what's gone before. By learning about history, we are learning all the time about ourselves. What could be more important than that!

If your GCSE course has shown *you* the importance of history, it will have achieved its main aim. If it has managed to do that, the chances are that you will have done well, both in the coursework and in the examination. There are bound to have been some problems. Bits of the course are likely to have proved difficult. But don't ever be put off by people (even teachers) who tell you that history isn't your subject, and don't get into the habit of thinking that yourself. History is one subject in which everyone can achieve something. This book will have been worth writing if it has helped *you* to find history more enjoyable – and at the same time, of course, to do better in your exam. Best of luck!

45.

OTTC Express UK
0895 444 383 .
—— A-2 Heathrow

55.7. 0208-759 0303 .
Area (w
01905 444 555 .
——

F45 .